BULIMIA —

HELP

ME, LORD!

BULIMIA — HELP ME, LORD!

By Molly Saunders

© Copyright 1988 — Molly Saunders

All rights reserved. This book is protected under the copyright laws of the United States of America. This book may not be copied or reprinted for commercial gain or profit. Short quotations and occasional page copying for personal or group study is permitted and encouraged. Just ask us for permission, we're not hard to get along with.

Destiny Image Publishers
P.O. Box 351
Shippensburg, PA 17257
"Speaking to the Purposes of God for this Generation"

ISBN 0-914903-53-5

For Worldwide Distribution
Printed in the U.S.A.

The Lord does not look at the things man looks at. Man looks at the outward appearance, but the Lord looks at the heart.

I Samuel 16:7

Affectionately dedicated to my husband,
Clyde, and to my daughters, Sherri and Becky.

Note: The following story is the actual account of the hardest but also the most rewarding year of my life. Many of the people who helped me along the road to recovery are not mentioned in this book, but they have a permanent place in my heart. The characters of Susan, Ann, Mr. Marsh and Nancy represent very real and special people, but their names were changed to protect their privacy. May God richly bless each of you.

Love,
Molly

"I thank my God every time I remember you." Philippians 1:3

ACKNOWLEDGMENTS

With all my heart I wish to gratefully acknowledge:

Cynthia Rowland, for the work she does in reaching out to people who suffer with bulimia.

Bud Harbin, for the many hours of guidance and for his wisdom in employing the best counseling tool available... The Holy Bible.

Pat and Debbie Hall, for loving me when I was unlovable and for allowing me to be a part of their lives.

Ida Snow, Kim Taylor, Linda Shira, and Mike DeWinter, for changing my story from scribbled notebook pages into a typed manuscript.

The National Anorexic Aid Society in Columbus, Ohio, for all their services, especially the free support groups.

The congregation of Central Church of Christ for their prayers, encouragement, hugs, and their powerful Christian influence on the lives of myself and my family.

FOREWORD

When Molly Saunders called me on the phone that day in August of 1985, I heard a very scared, timid voice asking me if I would consent to see and talk with her about her problem with bulimia. At that time she had been bulimic for eleven years, was bingeing and vomiting several times a week and felt totally out of control.

As if bulimia weren't enough, her struggle with diabetes made matters doubly hard. Her blood sugar was constantly too high or too low, a condition which gave her greater feelings of low self-esteem. Molly felt no good, worthless and ugly. She couldn't understand how anyone could like her, much less love her. Many times during the first few months of counseling she would cry and say, "My husband is so good and I'm so bad! I don't know why he loves me."

But Molly was determined. She began to believe in the possibility of her healing. She began to comprehend the love of God and the love of people. She began to have insight into what really makes a person valuable. The Bible says in I Samuel 16:7, ... "the Lord seeth not as man seeth; for man looketh on the outward appearance, but the Lord looketh on the heart." When Molly saw this truth and took it for herself, she began to see how she could be loved and lovable.

Long before Molly was free of her problems, she began reaching out to help others. She continues to do this as God leads. The change in her life is real. The story she has written is inspiring. I believe it will bless and encourage anyone who reads it.

Bud Harbin, LPC, NCC

CONTENTS

Chapter   **Page**

PART I — AM I INSANE?

1. That's Me! 3
2. I Can't Do It Alone 21
3. Why Am I Like This Anyway? 39

PART II — WHO IS THIS JESUS I THOUGHT I KNEW?

4. Soul Searching 63
5. Glimmer of Hope 77
6. Holiday Encounters 87

PART III — HE MAKES ALL THINGS BEAUTIFUL

7. Metamorphosis 101
8. Surely Not Me, Lord! 117
9. Going Public Is NO Picnic 127
10. Victory! 135
11. The Icing on the Cake 141

    IF YOU HAVE AN EATING DISORDER
    Anorexia Nervosa and Bulimia 153

PART I

AM I INSANE ?

1

That's Me!

I was busy driving along on my mail route on a hot, muggy day in June, 1985, when I glanced at my watch.

It was 10:10 a.m. "Darn," I thought. "I'm missing my favorite talk show!" I listened to Cincinnati's WLW MID-DAY program from ten a.m. to two p.m. every day while delivering the mail on my thirty-eight-mile rural route in Mount Vernon, Ohio. They had all kinds of guests. Sometimes there were authors and entertainers. They occasionally had a sex-therapist, and once they had even had a group of male strippers. It was never boring! I quickly turned the dial to 700 AM and continued on my mail route.

"Do you mean you actually did this every day?" the male radio host asked.

A woman's voice came on. "Yes, the bingeing and vomiting became my life: an addiction that I couldn't stop."

When I heard her words I almost drove my car into a mailbox. I stopped and listened intently. It was Cynthia Rowland, author of *The Monster Within*, a book dealing with bulimia. I listened as she tried to explain her struggle with bulimia to the radio host, who was apparently shocked by what he was hearing. For the next two hours she talked about her life: how she had binged and vomited, abused laxatives and become very good at lying to hide her habit. I focused my attention on every word she said, waiting to hear how she had stopped doing it.

As she explained the hardships and pain that she had experienced in trying to overcome bulimia, I cried. I went along looking at the letters through tears as I tried to deliver the mail, not wanting to miss a minute of the conversation. Cynthia Rowland had been bulimic for twelve years and had ended up in a hospital almost dead from the complications.

I will never forget that interview as long as I live. I had been bulimic for a long time, since I was seventeen years old. Now I was twenty-eight. I mentally counted off the years of self-abuse. I had been bingeing and vomiting for eleven years!

I thought about what I had been doing to myself all these years and NOBODY knew! I had never confided my problem with bulimia to anyone at all. I really didn't think I was doing anything wrong. In fact, until that day, I had rather enjoyed it.

I have been an insulin dependent diabetic since I was fifteen years old. At seventeen I got a job working in a bakery. I was excited about figuring out how to be able to eat donuts and not get sick, blood sugar-wise, and not get fat. I had gone along happy in my bingeing and vomiting all these years and it had never really even bothered me.

But today it did. This was the first time I had ever heard anyone talk about bulimia. I didn't even know that what I was doing had a name until Karen Carpenter died about a year earlier. I had read a newspaper article about how she had died from complications of anorexia nervosa. The article had also mentioned a similar eating disorder called bulimia. So I knew that what I was doing wasn't really normal, but it rarely crossed my mind that I should stop.

During the last two hours of the radio show they

opened the phone lines so people could call in and talk to Ms. Rowland. I couldn't believe all the calls she got. People called in and told all kinds of stories about their experiences with handling bulimia. When parents called in, worried about their daughters, she said, "They need help. They need love and support. It's very rare for anyone to get over bulimia on their own."

When the radio show was almost over they announced the address where you could write and get her book.

"If you or someone you know has a problem with bulimia, please, please get help. There are eating disorders treatment centers in several states. There are loving people who want to help. It's almost impossible to get over bulimia on your own." Ms. Rowland sounded like she was ready to cry. "It's so much easier to get over bulimia when you have the right kind of help. Send for my book. It has helped lots of people with bulimia and it can help you." She seemed to be pleading with the radio audience. She didn't know it but she had been talking to me for the four hours.

I hurriedly wrote down the name of her book and the address, folded the slip of paper and put it in my purse. I wasn't sure I wanted to send for it, but just in case I decided to, I would have the address.

I finished my mail route and went back to the post office to take care of the work I did every day in the afternoon. I could hardly keep my mind on my work. The radio program kept running through my mind.

"I have bulimia!" I was painfully aware of this thought that seemed to be pounding in my brain. I felt as though my head was going to explode from the agonizing statements that kept playing like a tape, over and over again. "If I don't stop this I could die! What am I doing to myself? Why am I like this? I am BULIMIC!!"

It was as if another person had invaded my body and

was slapping me, shaking me and screaming these awful thoughts at me. I couldn't think of anything else no matter how hard I tried.

When I got finished at work, I went over to my best friend Judy's house. We had been going on walks in the afternoon lately. It was good to get out, walking and talking about just anything that came to mind. My three-year-old daughter, Becky, went to a pre-school, and I didn't usually pick her up until later in the afternoon, about an hour before my husband, Clyde, came home.

When I got to Judy's she was waiting for me, ready to go on our walk. We had our usual route — up her street, downtown, around the public square and back. It was about a mile.

As we got started I thought about telling Judy about my bulimia. We had been friends for about eight years. Although Judy was ten years older than I, we had been like sisters ever since we had met. I had told her secrets that I had never told anyone, and I trusted her completely. But what about this? Did I dare tell her the horrible secret that I had been keeping for eleven years?

As we were walking along, chatting about this and that, I casually mentioned the radio program I had heard that day. I described in detail what Cynthia Rowland had talked about.

Judy had heard about anorexia but didn't know that there was another eating disorder called bulimia.

"This woman has written a book about bulimia. I'm thinking about sending for it," I said.

"Why?" asked Judy. "Do you know someone who does that?"

I wondered whether I should tell her. What would she think if she knew the truth? Would she still be my friend if she knew that I ate tons of food and spent many hours every week bingeing and throwing up? I decided to take the chance.

Nervously I began to tell her. "Well, I think I might have it... I'm not sure, but every once in a while when I eat so much that I'm miserable, I have made myself throw up. I've only done it a few times...not very often. I've probably only done it five or six times in my life." There were more lies in that statement than there was truth, but she didn't have to know the whole truth, did she?

I told her that since I was diabetic, throwing up was probably a smart thing for me to do when I ate a lot of stuff I wasn't supposed to have. If I kept a lot of extra food down then my blood sugar would be sky-high and I would be sick anyway.

"I don't really think I have bulimia though. That woman said when you start bingeing and purging it becomes like an addiction and you can't stop," I said. "I'm sure I can stop, I really haven't even done it very much. I just want to read the book. It might be interesting." I wondered if Judy could see the nervous little girl behind the mask I had put on. I wondered if she knew how afraid I was that anyone would find out about my secret life.

"I don't think you have it. After all, the woman on the radio said that she threw up five or six times a day, didn't she? Personally, I don't see how anyone could enjoy sticking their finger down their throat and making themselves throw up. I hate to throw up!" As Judy said this I cringed. If she knew how much I binged and vomited she would probably hate me. I had done it at her house many times before. Every time we had supper at her house I would make a trip to the bathroom, turn on the water to cover up the noise, stick my fingers down my throat, and make myself throw up.

"But if you do it even once in a while, maybe you

should send for the book. I don't think you have anything to worry about, though. Next time you eat too much just take more insulin. Your blood sugar won't go up, and you'll be fine." Judy said it so casually!

"She has no idea," I thought. For the first time that day I smiled. I was proud of myself for putting up such a good front and being such an expert liar. "I'll just send for the book and read it. Then I'll be able to stop this habit," I thought.

I got a money order and sent for *The Monster Within* the next day. I didn't want to write a check because I was afraid that when the cancelled check came back Clyde would see it and ask what book I was buying. I sent a letter with the book order saying that I was bulimic and needed help desperately.

After I sent for the book I went for three days without bingeing and purging. That was the longest amount of time I had abstained from my bulimic practices since I could remember. During that three days I had a hard time concentrating on my job, my family, or anything else I tried to focus my thoughts on. My mind was constantly battling with thoughts of food: "Don't eat! You won't be able to stop! Don't put anything in your mouth!"

I cut my insulin dose to almost nothing because I was trying hard to keep from eating anything. I bought a huge supply of carrots and celery to eat and six two-liter bottles of diet cola. I thought that if I kept my stomach full, I would have no desire to binge, but I was wrong.

After three days of very little sleep because of arguments in my brain, I was a nervous wreck. Deciding it wasn't worth the pain, I went and bought groceries, came home and involved myself in a full-blown binge. I decided that I wouldn't be able to stop bingeing and vomiting without the book I had sent for, so I might as well continue with bulimia until it arrived. During the two-week wait on the book I spent every free minute in a continuous cycle of grocery store, kitchen and bathroom.

"I might as well enjoy myself with the last weeks of freedom and when I read the book I'll find the magic formula that made the author well," I thought.

I got *The Monster Within* at the post office on Friday, June 28. I get my personal mail in the morning before I leave on my route. Since I had a few minutes to wait before I could leave, I decided to start reading it. I went to my mail-sorting case, which is back in an out-of-the-way corner, and ripped the package open. The cover of the book showed a drawing of a tiny woman lost in a jungle of giant cakes, pies and cookies.

"That's me!," I thought. The picture depicted just how I felt. Lost.

"GOD, PLEASE LET THIS BE THE ANSWER TO MY PRAYERS. HELP ME STOP THIS HORRIBLE THING I DO. I WANT TO BE A NORMAL PERSON."

I was just starting to read the book when Rhoda, a friend and co-worker, came over to talk. I didn't even hear her coming, I was so involved in reading the story.

"What are you reading, Molly?" she asked. I jumped! She had startled me, and I didn't want anyone to find out about me.

"Did you ever hear of anorexia? You know, people that starve themselves?" I quickly said.

Rhoda nodded.

"A real good friend of mine has a daughter who has bulimia. It's sort of like anorexia, but instead of starving she eats tons of food and then makes herself throw up," I lied. The lies rolled off my tongue like water off a duck's back. I didn't even have to think about it. I told Rhoda all about my friend's daughter (I named her Stephanie) and how she would eat bags of groceries a day and then throw up.

While we were talking, another friend, David, came

over. David is the minister of a small Baptist Church in addition to working at the post office. I explained to him about Stephanie, too.

"Her mom is about to lose her mind. She tries to stop Stephanie, but she can't. Stephanie can eat two boxes of cereal and a gallon of milk or a couple of boxes of donuts. I heard a woman on the radio a couple of weeks ago talking about this. I sent for the book to give to my friend."

David had heard of anorexia, but the word bulimia was totally foreign to him. Rhoda knew a little about it. We talked for a few minutes about what a shame it was that there was so much social pressure to be thin and that so many young girls were resorting to such drastic measures to stay that way.

In a few minutes it was time to leave for our mail routes, and as I said good-bye to Rhoda and David I mentally patted myself on the back for being such a good liar.

"Nobody will ever find out that it's really me. I'll read this book this afternoon and then I'll be able to stop this," I thought. Judy was the only person who knew, and she didn't really know the whole truth.

That afternoon I went home alone, and for the next two hours I read the book that I prayed would solve all my problems. It was hard reading the book through tears. The picture of what I was doing to myself was becoming more vivid with each page I turned.

Cynthia Rowland had gone through several months of hospital treatment and psychotherapy to get over bulimia. How could I get out of this overwhelming problem myself? She had help from trained professionals. Who was going to help me?

"I can't tell anyone how bad I really am," I thought. "I have to try to stop by myself."

Then I thought about Judy. I had told her secrets in the

That's Me! 11

past. I trusted her with feelings and things that I couldn't trust anyone else with. If I told her not to tell something that I had confided in her about, I knew she wouldn't. But what would she think about me if I told her the truth?

"GOD, I AM SO AWFUL. I EAT AND THROW UP EVERY DAY, AND I CAN'T STOP. I NEED TO TELL SOMEONE. PLEASE MAKE JUDY NOT HATE ME."

Saturday I woke up at 5:00. I kept thinking about my troubles and decided to tell Judy. I had to. I couldn't keep this problem to myself anymore.

After breakfast Clyde went to his mom's house to work on a car, and Becky was busy watching cartoons, so I wrote Judy a long letter. I told her that I had bulimia and that I really binge and purge every day. I said that if Clyde found out he would probably hate me. I asked her to help me and never tell anyone.

I wrote the letter in my bedroom, my tears falling on the page as I wrote. I heard the door slam and knew that Clyde was home so I folded the letter and put it in my pocket. Then I went to the bathroom to wash my face and put on some make-up so Clyde wouldn't know I had been crying.

Later that afternoon Clyde and Becky were watching T.V. in the living room. I took the book that I had gotten in the mail and hid it behind my back, telling Clyde that I needed to go see Judy for a few minutes.

"O.K., but don't be gone all afternoon," Clyde said as he glanced up from his T.V. show.

"Bye, Mom!" Becky called as I went out the door.

I was glad Judy was home alone. She was lying on her couch watching T.V. She must have known I was upset from the look on my face.

"What's wrong?" she asked.

I couldn't answer her. Tears welled up in my eyes and spilled out on my cheeks. Did I dare take the chance of losing my best friend? I handed her the book and the letter I had written. I couldn't watch her read it because I was so ashamed. I felt so ugly and disgusting. I went into her kitchen and sat down crying — actually crying out loud — sobbing. I don't remember ever having felt so much emotion in my life. This was the first time in eleven years of bingeing and vomiting that I had ever let anyone see the awful truth I had been hiding.

When Judy finished reading the letter she came into the kitchen and put her arm around my shoulder. When she did that I cried even more.

"I'm sorry. I'm so sorry," I sobbed. "I couldn't tell anyone. I tried to stop by myself, but I can't."

I stood up, and when Judy hugged me I clung to her and cried like a frightened child. After a few minutes we went into the living room, Judy got me a box of tissues, and I told her the whole story. Judy was bewildered by what I was telling her. She had known me for a long time. We had spent many hours together, had eaten lots of meals together, Judy never suspecting that I was going to the bathroom to throw up after we ate time after time.

Judy assured me that she loved me and would help in whatever way she could. She said she would read my book that afternoon.

"Maybe that will help me understand more about what's wrong with you."

"You can't tell Clyde. He'll hate me if he finds out," I pleaded with her to keep my secret. "I have told him so many lies about food that if he finds out he will probably leave me. Don't tell anyone — anyone at all!"

After a hug and a few more tears, I went home. I had been gone about two hours, and when I walked in the door Clyde said, "I thought you weren't going to be gone very long."

"I'm sorry. Judy had something she wanted to talk

about and it took longer than I thought it would," I said.

"What was so important that it took two hours?"

"It's something really bad, and I promised her I wouldn't tell anyone."

I gave him a kiss, and my answer seemed to satisfy him. I hoped that he couldn't tell that I had been crying.

That evening I went into the bathroom and locked the door. I had bought a small notebook and as my bath water ran into the tub, I sat on the toilet seat and started a diary.

Saturday, June 29, 1985. — Today I am trying to be my own therapist. I have just finished reading *The Monster Within*. It's a story about bulimia. Here are the symptoms I have:

1. Recurrent episodes of binge eating.
2. Termination of such episodes by self-induced vomiting.
3. Repeated attempts to lose weight by vomiting and laxatives.
4. Awareness that the eating pattern is abnormal and *fear of not being able to stop!!*

I think I can stop by myself. I can't tell anyone. Judy knows, but that's all. Why do I do this?

I will not throw up.
I will not throw up.
I will not throw up.
I will not throw up.
I will not throw up.

If I sit down and write about my feelings instead of eating, maybe I can figure out why I do this. I know I'm sick but I CAN overcome this. I will, I will, I will if it's the last thing I ever do. If I keep trying, I think I can make it. If I could stop for a month, I could quit then.

I went in the bedroom and put the diary in the drawer

of my nightstand, way back in the back, under everything else that was in there. I planned to write more but I didn't dare take a chance on Clyde's "catching me" writing. He might want to know what I was writing, and I would die if he knew about my bulimia. This was MY problem and I was going to get over it MYSELF.

After a quick bath I went into the living room to watch T.V. for a little while. I hoped Clyde couldn't see that anything was wrong with me. I sat on the couch beside him and gave him a kiss. I put my head on his shoulder and quickly wiped a silent tear off my cheek. I had so many thoughts and feelings running around inside me and was trying desperately to keep them from showing. This man that I loved was so good. He was a wonderful husband and father. We had been married for six years and had a good, solid marriage. If Clyde knew what was wrong with me though, I would probably lose him and Becky, the only good things in my miserable life.

Sunday, June 30. 5:00 A.M. — I couldn't sleep last night. I am trying to remember what has happened in my life to make me be this way. What is it? Why am I crazy? Why have I been eating like a pig and then throwing up for the past eleven years? I started it at the bakery when I was seventeen. I would eat cookies and cupcakes in secret and then go to the bathroom and throw up so my blood sugar wouldn't get too high.

I always wanted to be thin but I never have been. I weigh myself four or five times a day. But I never lose very much. My husband, Clyde, loves me very much. But he doesn't know a thing about this. I am real sneaky. I turn the water on so he won't hear me. I have done this everywhere — I can't help it. I am obsessed with being thin, and I don't know how to go about it. Even if I weighed 110 I would probably think I was fat. "PLEASE GOD, HELP ME THROUGH THIS DAY. DON'T LET ME LOSE CONTROL AGAIN." Love, Molly.

I had lots of ups and downs during the next week...so many questions and thoughts I was struggling with all by myself. Why am I like this? Why can't I think about good things instead of having all these fights in my brain?

I had two Mollys in my brain — a good Molly and a bad Molly. The good Molly was three inches high and had a toothpick for a sword. The bad Molly was six feet tall with all kinds of weapons — swords, guns, hand grenades. She was an ugly giant, so smug that she was in control. We would argue back and forth in my mind day after day, the typical argument going like this:

"Go ahead, Molly. Go buy donuts or ice cream. You don't have to tell anyone. No one will ever know."

"NO! I don't want to. I want to stop this behavior. I want to get over bulimia."

"But what's so wrong with it, Molly? You're not hurting anyone, are you? Look how long you've gotten away with it. You can stop next week. Go ahead!"

"NO! I can't eat. If I eat something I'm not supposed to have, I will go too far, and then I'll have to throw up. Please, please leave me alone. I don't want you in my life. Get out! Stop badgering me!"

"HA! HA! HA! You might as well give up! You know you'll never get over this. You are a miserable failure. You are worthless! You are ugly, fat and disgusting. The only pleasure you have in your miserable life you get from me. The foods that you binge on are so good. Sweet things that you won't be able to have if you change. If Clyde finds out he will leave you! Then you will have NOTHING! HA! HA! HA!"

The bad Molly was sure she would win the fight. The odds were in her favor. It seemed hopeless most of the time.

I wrote every day in my diary, recording my thoughts and writing down what I ate. Judy checked on me periodically to see how I was doing. I was afraid to eat very much, afraid that I would lose control again.

Night and day my mind was constantly battling, thinking about all the evil things I had done. It seemed like I had been bingeing and vomiting all my life. I was so afraid that I wasn't going to make it.

One week after I started the diary I was sure I was cured. I had gone the whole week without bingeing and purging.

> Sunday, July 7 — Well I've done it! I've gone a whole week without throwing up. Thank-You, God, for helping me through this week and for my friend, Judy. I think I'm going to be O.K! — Molly

That very day the bad Molly took control again, and I binged that night. I had a long list of foods — a milkshake, a box of cookies, two hamburgers, two pieces of bread and jelly and half a package of lunch meat. Then I went and threw up.

> Monday, July 8 — It's starting again! I feel terrible about what I did last night. Once I started I couldn't stop. I just kept eating and eating. I hate what I have done. I wish I could have stopped with just one cookie. It's like I went crazy! I'm going to stay on my diet today if it kills me. I must be patient and keep trying. How much food have I wasted over the past eleven years, eating and throwing up? God probably hates me. His little children are starving to death in Africa because they don't have any money or food. And here I am still throwing food down the toilet, even after I said I wouldn't do it anymore. How many times can God forgive that? Oh, I am so bad. I

was a failure last night. I hate myself for losing control again. I must stop this craziness.

The rest of July was very traumatic. My diary was full of hurtful words — disgusting, failure, loser, fat, ugly, worthless, on and on and on. I was describing myself. On the days that I wasn't able to control my eating I was a failure. If I ate one cookie I considered that I had ruined that day and even if I didn't throw up I still felt defeated. My diary was filled with broken promises to do better and then beating myself down for not being able to keep them. Life was a lot better when I was just eating and throwing up and not letting it bother me.

I really did want to give up and go back to bulimia, but Judy knew about me and kept checking on me. She couldn't understand why I binged and purged. She just loved me, and I had to stop doing this for her.

Before long I was so disgusted by my weakness and failures that I couldn't tell the truth even to myself. It was so hard to read about my binges and the vomiting in black and white. The bad Molly told me that if I didn't write it down or tell Judy, it would be like it didn't happen.

Saturday, August 3 — I have been slipping back to my old evil habits. I have eaten and thrown up more times than I have written in this diary. Yesterday I did it twice. I have to admit it and keep writing things down. What good does it do to write in here and not tell the truth? God knows what I do. He wants me to stop it, so why can't I?

I wonder if I will ever stop. I want to, but I must not want it bad enough. I am devious, conniving, sneaky and disgusting. I am no good. I have no guts. I have tried, but I have failed. How can I go on living like this?

I got a letter from our church yesterday. They

have assigned us an elder that we are supposed to go to if we need to talk to anyone. That's a laugh. He would flip out if he knew what I did. They probably wouldn't allow someone as terrible as me in the church if they knew how I really was.

I am like a drug addict or an alcoholic. But I don't want to be, so once again I promise to always tell the truth in this diary and stop pigging out and throwing up.

Judy had been reading my diary every day, checking up on me. I wanted her to read it so she would be proud of me on days I was good and didn't throw up. She had assured me of her love, and I knew that she really meant it.

Becky had spent Friday night at Judy's because Clyde and I both had to work on Saturday. After work I drove into Judy's driveway and sat in the car, thinking about whether to let her read the diary today. I was ashamed for throwing up and not telling her, and I felt intense anger at myself for not having enough guts to admit my failures.

Judy came out to the car and told me that Becky was taking a nap. When she saw me holding the diary, she got in the car to read it. She finished reading, slammed the diary shut and threw it onto the dashboard of my car.

"What's the use of trying to help?" she said angrily. "Are you trying to kill yourself? Think about that baby of yours! What kind of a mother are you, anyway? I can't help you if you're going to lie to me!"

As soon as she said it I could tell she was sorry. Tears streamed down my cheeks as she tried to apologize.

"I'm sorry, Molly. I didn't mean it. I DO want to help you. I just don't know what to do. I can't understand how anyone could eat and then throw up. I wish I knew what to do to make you stop."

"So do I!" I cried. "Do you think I want to be this way? I hate it! I hate myself for doing it! Every time I think I'm over it I screw up again! I don't know what to do! If I don't get better soon I'm going to kill myself! You and Clyde and Becky would be better off without me anyway!"

"Stop it!" Judy said. "You will get over this, but maybe it's time you looked somewhere else for help. I'm not a shrink. I can't figure it out, but there has to be someone around who can help you."

I didn't want to admit it, but I had a sinking feeling that she was right.

2

I Can't Do It Alone

On Monday, August 12, I couldn't handle it anymore. I had binged and vomited several times over the weekend; nothing I tried could stop the endless arguments in my brain. I felt that if I didn't find help soon I would die.

After I got off work I went to the Public Library in Mt. Vernon and got out the phone book for Columbus, Ohio. Surely there would be someone there who knew what was wrong with me. Columbus is about an hour's drive from Mt. Vernon, and I thought I would be safe if I went that far away; there would be little chance of Clyde's finding out why I was going.

I opened the heavy directory to the Yellow Pages and looked under PSYCHOLOGISTS. There were so many! How could I find one who knew about bulimia? I looked under HYPNOSIS. There! "EATING BEHAVIOR MODIFICATION — OVERCOME THE DESIRE TO OVEREAT."

That's what I had, wasn't it? I couldn't stop eating once I got started — maybe hypnosis would help. I wrote down the phone number and went home to call them.

"Yes, I overeat — bags of groceries at a time; then I make myself throw up. I've tried to stop, but I can't. It's called bulimia. Have you ever heard of it?"

The lady on the other end of the phone sounded bewildered.

"Yes, I have heard of bulimia . . . just a minute." Then

she put her hand over the phone and I could make out the muffled sounds of her discussing my problem with someone else. After a minute or so she came back on the phone.

"Hello? Can I have your name and number? I'll talk to Dr. Smith in a few minutes and get back to you."

"Do you promise to call me right back? I can't wait much longer. I really can't! Please promise me you'll call right away," I begged.

"I promise I will, Honey," she answered in a concerned voice.

I hung up the phone and paced back and forth in the kitchen, waiting for her call. Five minutes went by — no call. I picked up the receiver to see if someone was on the other party line. Hearing the dial tone I quickly hung up again. After a few minutes of pacing I heard the phone ring.

"Hello?"

"Hello. Is this Molly?"

"Yes."

"I'm sorry, Dr. Smith doesn't deal with anorexia or bulimia...but I have some information about where you can call for help." She gave me the phone number of a place called "The Center for the Treatment of Eating Disorders" in Westerville.

I called there and explained that I was bulimic and inquired about the treatment. I wasn't prepared for the cost involved in psychotherapy. I was informed that there were options — reduced rates for low incomes, or perhaps my insurance would cover some of the cost. I didn't see how I could go, without Clyde's finding out.

"I'm sorry, but my husband doesn't know I even have bulimia. I can't tell him or spend that kind of money without his finding out." My trembling voice turned into sobs.

I Can't Do It Alone 23

"Wait. Don't hang up. Just a minute. I have a list of places that deal with eating disorders. Let me see if there are any closer to Mt. Vernon or any less expensive...Here's a listing for the Nazarene College in Mt. Vernon. Do you know where that is?"

When I told her that I lived only three blocks from the college, she told me to call there.

"We also have a free support group in Columbus. It's at the Bridge Counseling Center on Karl Road. It meets on the second and fourth Tuesdays of each month. In fact, they're meeting tomorrow night." She gave me the directions and I hung up, drained of emotion from the past half hour of searching for help.

What would Clyde think if I went to Columbus by myself on a Tuesday evening? It was a little over an hour's drive away, and I probably wouldn't be home much before ten o'clock. What story could I make up this time that he would believe?

I thought Clyde was getting suspicious. I realize now that I had been dropping hints and trying to leave evidence around for him to find. I guess I wanted to get caught. I had asked him questions like: "Would you love me no matter what I did? If I really did something terrible, would you forgive me and love me?"

I had left the book *The Monster Within* on the table a couple of times, hoping he would take notice of it. I guess he just figured that it was another of the many books I had bought on how to lose weight. He was never too interested in my devices to try to become thinner.

"If he knew the truth, he would probably leave me," was one of my frequent thoughts. But another part of me wanted to tell him. I just didn't know what to do. I checked the time and, to my surprise, saw that it was only 3:30. Clyde wouldn't be home for two more hours!

"Go see what there is to eat!" the bad Molly whispered in my brain. "It won't hurt if you have a bowl of cereal."

What started out with a bowl of cereal turned into a whole box and a frantic search for more — cookies, ice cream, toast and peanut butter and a half gallon of milk to wash it all down.

I went to the bathroom and made myself throw up — the very thing that I had promised over and over never to do again.

I flushed the toilet and looked at myself in the mirror. The skin around my eyes had little red splotches; my face was covered with ugly blemishes, and my hair was a mess.

"Why did you do it?" I angrily asked myself. "You are weak! You can't even control what you eat. Clyde won't love you anymore if you tell him. You can try all you want, but you'll never change!"

I continued to stare at my disgusting self. "Clyde loves me," I tried to tell myself. "There must be something good in me somewhere." But right then all I could see was ugly, fat, horrible me.

It was a little after 4:00 by this time, and I decided I had better go get Becky at school. I would have to stop at the store to replace all the food I had eaten, so I got some money and went to my desk to get my purse.

There was a letter on my desk from Clyde! I hadn't noticed it when I came in. I picked it up with shaking hands and began to read.

> Molly,
> I don't know what's been bothering you lately, but I know you're hiding something from me. What are you doing behind my back? All I know is that when two people are married, they should love each other and be faithful to each other. If there is another man in your life I want to know. I can't stand the thought

of you cheating on me. I hope I'm wrong. Don't lie to me. — Clyde.

He thought I was having an affair! How could he even think that? But what else could he think? It was true, I *had* been acting awfully strange lately. Here I was, married to a wonderful man, and he thought I was having an affair!

I loved Clyde with all of my heart. In my whole married life I had never once thought of being unfaithful. There were a lot of things I had done in my life that I was ashamed of, but not this. Besides, I felt so ugly, fat and dumb that even if I had wanted another man's attention I doubted if anyone would be interested. It was a miracle that Clyde loved me. He was so good — I was nothing but bad through and through.

I decided right then that tonight I was going to tell him. All this time I thought I was just hurting myself. That was O.K., but I couldn't bear to hurt Clyde by lying to him any more.

That evening when Clyde came home, I was waiting for him by the door. Fighting back tears, I said that I loved him and would tell him what was going on after supper. I could see the hurt in his eyes. The fear of what I was going to tell him was tearing him apart.

Supper was very tense. Becky kept her constant chatter going, but neither Clyde nor I paid very much attention to her. Clyde was silent. He wouldn't even look at me.

He had already been through an agonizing divorce. Was I going to lay something on him to make him go through that again? How could I explain that I was addicted to bingeing and throwing up? What words could I use to make him understand what I was going through? He was so good; he never lied to me like I had lied to him. Would he forgive me? Would he ever be able to love me after I told him my horrible secret?

As I was clearing away the dishes, a knock came at the door.

"Becky! Come and see me!" It was Judy. Becky ran to her and Judy carried her into the kitchen.

"Hi there," she said in a cheerful voice. "How are you doing?"

I looked at her, and tears welled up in my eyes. I couldn't find any words. Judy sent Becky outside to play and came back into the kitchen. She put her arm around my shoulders and asked me what was wrong.

"I can't handle this any more, Judy. Clyde thinks I'm having an affair," I whispered. Clyde was in the living room, and I didn't want him to hear. I told Judy about the support group in Columbus the next night.

"I have to tell Clyde. I can't stand lying to him anymore. Will you take Becky somewhere for awhile?"

"Of course I will," said Judy. "I think you're right —Clyde needs to know. If you want to go to that support group tomorrow night, I'll go with you. I wish I knew what to say to make this easier for you."

"Thanks. Just take Becky and keep your fingers crossed. I don't know how he's going to take it." I dried my tears and went out the front door with Judy. We watched Becky swinging on the swing-set. When she saw Judy and me standing at the door, she ran across the yard to us.

"Do you want to go with me and get some ice cream, Becky?" Judy asked.

"Yea! Can I, Mom?" Becky asked with a huge smile. I picked her up, and she wrapped her arms around me and gave me a kiss. "Please, Mom. I'll be good; I promise!"

I nodded and tried to put on a convincing smile.

"God, why does this beautiful child have such a terrible mother?" I thought. I put Becky down, and Judy reached for my hand, giving it a squeeze.

"Do you think an hour will be long enough?" Judy asked me.

"I don't think it will take Clyde that long to say he hates me," I whispered.

"Oh, don't be stupid!" Judy said. "He won't understand it, but he loves you. You can't let him think you have a lover!"

"I know. Bring her back in an hour. That should be long enough," I said. "Thanks."

I turned around to go back in the house and caught sight of Clyde walking from the window. He had been standing there watching us. I wondered what was going on in his mind. It was ironic: we were both scared but for two different reasons. Clyde was scared of finding out that I had a lover. I was scared of telling him the truth. Bingeing and throwing up was something that I knew would be very difficult to explain.

I went in the house and straight to the bedroom. I got my diary and the book *The Monster Within* and took them to the dining room.

"Will you come out here?" I said as I sat down at the table.

Clyde came into the dining room and just stood there staring at me. There was a look of anger on his face that I had never seen. In all our married life Clyde had never hurt me. In fact, people who knew me got tired of my bragging about this marvelous husband of mine. Now he was standing there with his jaw set, as if he were bracing himself for the awful news I was about to tell him.

"Will you please come over here and sit down?" I asked him after a few tense minutes of silence.

He came over, pulled the chair away from the table about two feet and sat down, saying nothing. He wouldn't even sit at the table with me.

"I have to tell you something that I've been keeping a secret for a long time," I began, wondering if our marriage would ever make it through the night. "But it isn't what you think." I was trying very hard to keep my voice steady, but inside I was shaking like a leaf.

"I have something wrong with me. I kept it a secret for a long time because I was afraid you wouldn't love me anymore if you found out."

I paused, waiting for Clyde to say something. I searched his face, looking for some sign of emotion. He just glared at me, silent.

"I love you, Honey," I said. "Don't you believe me?"

Nothing.

"I have a disease called bulimia. I heard a woman talking about it on the radio about a month ago, and I sent for this book." I slid the book over in front of Clyde, and he looked down at it, not even picking it up. His expression slowly changed from one of anger to one of confusion.

"It's an addiction to eating lots of food and then throwing up. I'm not the only one that does this — there are lots of people that do it. I tried to stop all by myself, but I can't. This book says that people like me have a problem that needs professional help. This lady was this way for twelve years, and she almost died. She needed help from psychologists, and she got so bad that she ended up in the hospital." I was talking very fast now, my sentences running together in an attempt to get all the explaining over with.

I could tell that Clyde was having a hard time understanding. How could he? I didn't fully understand it myself.

I reached back over and picked up the untouched book. I opened it to the last few pages, which contained an explanation about bulimia, and held it out to Clyde. He waited a minute, then took the book out of my hands and began to read.

"I called around to find out where the doctors were that treated this, but they cost a lot of money." I had been crying during this one-sided conversation; the napkin holder on the table was almost empty, and a pile of wadded up, soggy ones was growing on the table before me.

"Why do I always cry like this?" I thought. "Clyde hates it when I cry."

I watched Clyde's face as he read down the list of symptoms in the book. I had underlined the words "self-induced vomiting" and "fear of not being able to stop" with a pencil and drawn arrows and exclamation points behind the sentences. I guess I thought that drawing attention to how awful I was would make me stop bingeing and vomiting. My worst fear, the fear of Clyde's finding out my horrible secret, was coming true.

I searched Clyde's face for some sign that he still loved me. As he read, his eyes paused at certain points and then continued. When he finished the list, he closed the book, leaned back on his chair and shut his eyes. It was as if he were trying to shut out the awful truth he was hearing.

"I found out about a support group in Columbus that's free," I said. "It's tomorrow night. Judy said she'll go with me. She's the only one that knows about this."

I tried to figure out what Clyde was thinking. Where were the arms that had comforted me through burnt suppers, broken dishes and other minor tragedies of marriage? He was shocked! The wife that he thought he knew was revealing a life that she had kept secret for the six years we had been married. I wondered if it would have been better if I did have a lover. I was so ashamed.

In my mind the bad Molly laughed and pointed a long finger at me. "GUILTY! GUILTY! GUILTY!" she jeered. "HA! HA! HA!" After a long silence I whispered,

"Don't you have anything to say?"

"What do you want me to say?" Clyde asked in a harsh voice that was unfamiliar to me.

"That you still love me?" I said quietly.

Clyde didn't answer. Instead he got up, pushed his chair back in and walked stiffly into the living room.

"He hates me! I knew he would. Oh, why was I ever born? He doesn't deserve a wife like me," I thought. Tears ran down my cheeks and fell on the table. I looked hopelessly at the pile of napkins on the table and tried hard to stop crying. I wished Clyde would do something! Even if he came and hit me or yelled at me it would be better than this; at least I would know where I stood.

I cleaned off the table and went into the bathroom to wash my face. I looked at myself in the mirror. My eyes were red from crying, and I wondered if I would make it through the night.

I was hurt by Clyde's reaction, but what could I expect? Could I really expect him to say, "Honey, I love you, and I'm still glad you're my wife?" How could anyone love such a loathsome creature as myself?

"Hi, Dad! Judy and I got ice cream cones! I didn't eat all mine. It was too cold. Is that O.K?" Becky ran into the house, the front door slamming behind her. She didn't wait for an answer from Clyde. Instead she saw the bathroom light on and came looking for me. "Can you wash me, Mom? I'm a little bit dirty."

I turned to look at her and couldn't help smiling. She had chocolate ice cream all over her face, on her hands and down the front of her shirt.

Judy followed her into the bathroom. "Sorry, I didn't mean to let her get so dirty. Can you believe I didn't have any napkins in my car?" she said.

As I washed Becky up, Judy asked me, "Well, what did he say?"

I Can't Do It Alone 31

I sent Becky outside to play before I answered her.

"Did you see him when you came in? Where is he?" I asked. I didn't want Clyde to hear us talking about him.

"He went outside when we came in," Judy said. "I don't know where he went."

"He didn't say anything. He just looks at me like he hates me!" I said, starting to cry again.

"He doesn't hate you," Judy said. "He probably doesn't know how he feels. He just needs to think about what you told him. Give him a little time."

"Thanks," I said. "And thanks for taking Becky for ice cream."

"What are friends for?" she said, giving me a hug. "But listen, I have to go. George is waiting for me. Call me if you need me."

George was Judy's husband. They had been married only about a year. The memory of their wedding became clear in my mind. I had been Judy's matron of honor, and Clyde had been George's best man. Remembering the photographs of the four of us — Judy and I dressed in our long dresses and Clyde and George in their sharp looking suits — made me wish for the happier days. Those were the days when my bulimia was my own secret and wasn't causing anybody any problems.

I went outside, looking for Becky and Clyde. Becky was swinging, as usual, and Clyde was sitting at the picnic table, his back to the house. It was beginning to get dark so I brought Becky in and put her to bed.

"I love you, Mom," Becky said as she gave me a hug and crawled under the covers. "See you when we get up."

I turned off her light and walked slowly out of the bedroom. Becky was so innocent. She didn't have any idea what was going on.

"OH, GOD, I AM SO TERRIBLE! THE PEOPLE WHO LOVE ME ARE FINDING OUT WHAT I REALLY AM. I'M SO ASHAMED."

I went to look for Clyde. It was dark now. I could see him still sitting at the picnic table, the street light shining on his head, which was buried in his hands as if he were praying.

"Go find something to eat, Molly! He's not going to come in and sleep with you tonight! He might never sleep with you again!" The bad Molly was after me again. "You might as well eat! You know it's the only thing you really enjoy!"

"No!" I thought. "I'm not going to eat any more tonight. I have to show Clyde that I'm trying to stop this."

I went to bed alone and just lay there staring up at the ceiling, my mind in total chaos. I was waiting, hoping, but not really believing, that Clyde would come in and tell me he loved me and everything would be all right.

I don't know how long it was before Clyde came in. I must have fallen asleep, but I woke up when the bathroom light came on. Clyde came in and sat on the edge of the bed.

"I don't understand what's wrong with you," he said slowly, "but I do love you and I want you to get better. If it costs money — I don't care how much — we'll figure out a way."

"He loves me! He loves me!" I thought. The words I had been hoping for were being spoken. I sat up and put my arms around his neck.

"I'm sorry I kept it from you for so long. I didn't know what you would say." My tears were starting again — this time tears of relief. "As long as you love me I know I'll be all right."

"I know you will, Honey," Clyde said. When we went to bed Clyde's strong arms were around me once again, protecting me from whatever evil was causing me all this pain. I drifted into a weary, yet hopeful sleep.

The next day was Tuesday, August 13. All through the day I had mind fights about whether to go to the free support group or not. I was torn between wanting an instant cure and a fear that anyone else would have to know about my secret before I could get any better. I had already told Clyde and Judy, and I wasn't sure that I wanted anyone else to see the real me.

"But the group is in Columbus," I told myself. "Nobody there will know me. If they hate me I won't care because I won't have to see them again. And maybe it will help. It certainly can't hurt."

I tried to give myself pep talks all day. When I got done working I was almost glad I was going. Whatever happened, nothing could be as bad as what I had gone through the night before when I had told Clyde about my bulimia.

Judy and I left for Columbus early in the afternoon. We had decided to leave early and stop for supper on the way.

When we got to Columbus and stopped at a fast food restaurant near the support group, I wondered how Judy would act while we were eating. I was very uncomfortable eating with her now that she knew my secret. I was afraid that she would watch every bite that I put into my mouth.

I ordered a salad — a "safe" food. I never threw up if I was able to stop at eating just a salad. I had a feeling of uneasiness while I ate, but I made it through my salad without suffering too much anxiety. During the meal Judy and I exchanged ideas about what we thought the group would be like. We were able to chat and even laugh like we always had.

When we were finished I told Judy that I was going to the restroom, and she got up and followed me. The restroom was small, with no dividing wall between the stool and the sink. When I went in and turned to shut the door, Judy pushed the door open and followed me right in!

"I'm just going to use the restroom, Judy," I said.

"And I just want to make sure you use it for what it's supposed to be used for!" Judy came in, shut the door and stood in front of the mirror combing her hair and watching me out of the corner of her eye.

"I guess I don't blame her," I thought. "I don't even trust myself. Maybe I do need a babysitter." I felt so humiliated that I couldn't even be trusted to go to the bathroom alone.

Judy and I left the restaurant and drove to the counseling center where the support group meeting was supposed to be. When we arrived, the parking lot was practically empty. It was an older two-story house that had been converted into offices — not really what I had expected. I had pictured a big, hospital-looking building. After all, this place was for sick people, wasn't it?

When we went in the front door, the receptionist politely informed us that we were in the wrong building and directed us to the cement block building in back of the main offices.

I followed Judy into a large room with about twenty chairs arranged in a circle. There was a small table with newsletters containing information about eating disorders right by the door, and Judy and I each picked one up.

I didn't really want to sit in the circle. All of the chairs were empty but one, which was occupied by a woman whom I guessed to be in her late twenties, apparently absorbed in a magazine she was reading. When she heard us come into the room she looked up at us, smiled and said, "Hi!" and continued with her reading.

I stood there, embarrassed, as if the hardest decision

I Can't Do It Alone 35

I'd ever had to make was deciding where to sit. I noticed three chairs outside the circle, back against the wall by a pop machine. I took hold of Judy's arm and practically dragged her to them, wanting to be out of the way and hoping nobody would notice me.

While Judy read the newsletter she had picked up I studied the woman seated in the circle of chairs, who was seemingly unaware of our presence.

I had always felt inferior to people who were thinner and more beautiful than I was. Although this woman was not strikingly beautiful in appearance she was quite a bit thinner than I, which made me uneasy in her presence. I wondered if she had an eating disorder. I mean, you couldn't tell; this woman looked normal! I tried to picture what other people with bulimia looked like and decided that I would probably be the fattest, ugliest one there.

More people came in, one or two at a time, and soon all the chairs were full. Some of the women, like me, sat quietly, nervously staring at the floor. Others who had obviously been there before and knew each other were busy talking cheerfully as if they were actually having a good time.

I kept looking at my watch, wondering when the meeting was going to start. It was supposed to begin at 7:00. At 7:10 I whispered to Judy, "If they're not going to start on time, I'm leaving."

I was about to get up when the door opened once again. Five women filed into the room, and the people who had been talking suddenly became silent. Everyone looked in their direction, and a middle aged, motherly woman with a quiet manner and a friendly smile began to speak.

"Hello, my name is Arline Iannicello, and I am the program director for this support group of the National Anorexic Aid Society. I'm the facilitator for the family and friends' group, and we have a group for those with anorexia and one for those with bulimia." She looked at the other women who had come in with her and said, "Will you introduce yourselves, please?"

"I'm Terri," said one of the women.

"And I'm Tricia," said another. "We facilitate the bulimic support group. It's in the other building, so if you would follow us..."

I just sat there as they were followed out the door by several women, including the lady who had been busy reading when we first came in.

"That's you," Judy said quietly. I wanted to go, but my feet felt numb, and I didn't move.

"Go on!" she whispered in my ear, giving me a nudge with her elbow.

I hurriedly got to my feet and followed the last of the women to the second floor of the main building.

The group was very informal. Terri and Tricia were warm, caring individuals, professional yet friendly. I could sense true compassion from them for each person in the group.

The women began talking, each casually telling their names and how long they had been bulimic. At first I was very uncomfortable, but as they began sharing their experiences I felt more at ease.

I told the group about the mind fights that I had. As I described the enormous, powerful bad Molly and the tiny, feeble good Molly I saw heads nodding in agreement. I felt a great weight being lifted from my shoulders. At last I was able to discuss what I was going through with people who knew exactly what I was talking about!

Near the end of the meeting I was filled with new thoughts and ideas. I also had mixed emotions about what I had learned. Some of the women had been going to professional therapists for various lengths of time, a couple of them longer than a year. A year seemed like an awfully long time to me. I had thought that if I went for a month without bingeing and purging I could stop forever, but now I wasn't sure. The woman that I had first seen when I came in had been bulimic for eighteen years. I felt both hopeful and discouraged at the same time.

Tricia looked at the clock and announced that it was time to wind up the meeting.

"We meet on the second and fourth Tuesdays of each month," she said. "The group can be really helpful, but we also recommend individual counseling — it's very important." Then, looking directly at me, she continued. "We have information about where counseling is available if you'll see Terri or me afterwards."

As the women began to leave, I told Terri and Tricia that I had found out about a therapist in Mt. Vernon at the Nazarene College. They both urged me to call and stressed the importance of finding a therapist who was familiar with the complications of bulimia.

"I will," I promised. "I'll call the college tomorrow."

Terri touched me lightly on the arm as I turned to go. "I'm really glad you came, Molly. It takes a lot of courage to make the first step, but you've done it. I hope you'll come back. We really do care."

Judy and I discussed what we had learned from the groups on the way back to Mt. Vernon. When I got home around 10:00 I was exhausted, both physically and emotionally.

The light was on in the living room, and I hoped that Clyde was still up so I could talk to him about what I had learned at the support group. I still wasn't sure how he felt about me. He had assured me last night that he still loved me and would help any way he could, but I knew that I had hurt him by lying to him all these years.

The living room was empty, and I knew that Clyde had gone to bed. I put my purse away, and as I walked into the dining room, I stopped short. On the table was a vase containing six red carnations, and there was an envelope standing up against the vase!

My heart leaped as my shaking hands carefully opened the envelope. The get-well card inside had a comical drawing of a white rabbit dressed in a tuxedo. The rabbit was holding in one paw a magician's wand and in the other, an inverted top hat with a rainbow shooting up out of it. Inside was written:

"Honey, I love you no matter what. I want to help you get well. Hope the meeting helped. All my love, Clyde."

3

Why Am I Like This Anyway?

On Wednesday, August 14, I was determined to call Nazarene College and find out about their program for treating people with bulimia. I was still scared about telling anyone else, but I knew from the support group meeting last night that I probably couldn't get over bulimia on my own.

I had stifling feelings of guilt and shame that I couldn't shake off, no matter how hard I tried.

"Only crazy people go to see a shrink... I guess I am crazy though... nobody in their right mind would eat tons of food and then throw up!" I was bombarded by these nagging thoughts throughout the day. I envisioned the hideous bad Molly dancing in my brain singing, "Crazy! Crazy! HA! HA! HA! You are really crazy!"

I went home after work and called the college as soon as I got in the door. I had given Clyde my word that I would call, and I just couldn't break my promises to him anymore.

I forced myself to dial the number and explain my problem to the college phone operator. When I told her that I needed to talk to someone who took care of bulimia patients, she hit me with some disturbing news.

"I'm sorry; the counseling office is closed during the summer and won't be open until September when school starts again."

September! Although it was only three weeks away it seemed like an eternity to me.

"I don't know if I can wait until September. I'm sorry to lay all this on you but... I just... never mind. I guess I can wait till then. Thanks anyway," I told her, trying to keep my voice steady.

"Wait, the counselor's name is Bud Harbin. I think he does some counseling during the summer, but I'm not sure he could work you in." I knew she sensed the urgency in my voice. "I could give you his number..."

I scribbled the number on my tablet and hung up, wondering what I would say when I got him on the phone.

After a few minutes of mentally rehearsing what I planned to say, I dialed the number, sort of hoping he wouldn't be home. A man answered, and I asked him if I could speak to Bud Harbin.

"This is Bud," he said in a deep voice. "What can I do for you?"

I admitted to him that I was bulimic, told him my name and asked if he would be able to help me.

"Well, I have counseled with some bulimic girls at the college. How old are you, Molly?"

"Twenty-eight."

"And how long have you been bulimic?"

"About eleven years."

"Hmm... How tall are you, and how much do you weigh?"

"I'm 5'7" and weigh around 135."

"How many times a day do you vomit?"

Vomit! I hated that word with a passion! It sounded so ugly. I had done it thousands of times in the past, but to talk about it to a total stranger was almost more than I could stand. If I hadn't promised Clyde that I would call I would have hung up right then.

I wearily told him that I used to do it several times a day but now was trying, without much success, to stop.

We talked a few agonizing minutes more, and Mr. Harbin said he could see me on Friday afternoon.

After writing the directions to Mr. Harbin's house on my tablet I thanked him and hung up. Bud Harbin seemed very direct and perhaps a bit harsh. I wondered if I would be able to survive talking with this man face to face.

Friday morning I woke up at 4:00 a.m. Unable to get back to sleep I got up quietly so I wouldn't wake Clyde. My reflection in the mirror looked awful. My eyes were bloodshot from the lack of sleep I had experienced since this fight had begun a month and a half before. I felt so ugly I couldn't even stand to look at myself anymore.

I got my ever-present diary out and began to write, hoping that soon I would be free of bulimia and not have to keep writing down my feelings and failures.

Friday, August 16 — Today is the day I go to see Bud Harbin. I'm very nervous about it. I don't want to go, but I have to. Everyone is finding out what a terrible person I am. I'm so ashamed. I wonder what Mr. Harbin will say to me. Will he look at me like I'm crazy?

Last night I had a good supper, but I wanted to eat something else. I kept picturing a big chocolate sundae — gobs of whipped cream, nuts and lots of chocolate sauce. I wanted it so badly but I can't have even a bite or I'll lose control. I tried to think about other things, but since I've tried to stop this awful habit all I think about is food. I'm scared about this afternoon. I know my heart will be racing when I get to Mr. Harbin's house. What will I tell him? What will he ask *ME*? Questions keep going over and over in my mind. Please, God, get me through this day.

After finishing up at the Post Office around 3:00, I went home to get ready for my 4:00 appointment with Mr.

Harbin. Judy was going to pick Becky up at pre-school for me and watch her until I got done. It took me a long time to decide what to wear. I tried on three or four different T-shirts, but they all had pictures or sayings on them — nothing really suitable for seeing a shrink. I finally decided on jeans and a yellow tank top. I grabbed my diary on the way out, thinking that Mr. Harbin might want to read it so he could figure out what was wrong with me.

I arrived at Mr. Harbin's house five minutes early. A teenage girl answered the door, and when I told her my name she looked confused.

"Dad said the appointment was for 4:30, but you can come in and wait for him."

I wanted to die of embarrassment as I followed her into a large, carpeted room in the basement. There was a sofa and a couple of chairs on one side of the room. I uneasily sat down on the edge of the sofa.

"Here, I'll turn the T.V. on for you," the girl said off-handedly. "You can change the channel if you want." She flipped the T.V. set on, then left, closing the door behind her.

"GOD, I AM SO STUPID! I WAS SUPPOSED TO BE HERE AT 4:30, NOT 4:00! NOW I'LL HAVE TO SIT HERE FOR HALF AN HOUR. I WISH I COULD DIE!"

I tried to watch the T.V. and keep my mind off the impending confrontation between me and the unknown Bud Harbin. The show was a rerun of an old sit-com, but right now, try as I might, I couldn't find anything funny. I kept looking at my watch every three or four minutes, wishing I had listened better on the phone. By the time 4:30 arrived my palms were sweaty, and my head was beginning to ache. Would this day ever come to an end?

The door opened, and a tall, slender man with graying hair walked in. Bud Harbin was carrying a manila folder in one hand, and he held out his other hand for me to shake as he smiled and introduced himself. He sat in the chair across from me and opened the folder.

The first few minutes of conversation were very tense as I began to divulge my secret life to this man. As we talked I described in detail my secretive life, telling him everything I could think of as if trying to shock him with how awful I was.

He seemed to know all about bulimia and didn't appear shocked in the least by what I had told him. He directed the conversation to my religious background, all the while making notes in his folder.

Yes, I was a Christian; I had been raised going to church and had accepted Christ as my Saviour when I was thirteen. I knew it wasn't GOD's fault that I was bulimic; I had gotten into this mess all by myself. I wasn't even sure that there was a God anymore. If there was He certainly couldn't love me. I had prayed many prayers in the past six weeks, asking Him to take away the desire to binge and purge. I figured I must not be good enough for God to answer my prayers because I seemed to get worse as each day went by. I told Mr. Harbin that I still went to the same church that I had grown up in. Well, once in a while anyway. Some of the people there were pretty nice, but somehow I didn't quite fit in. I wished Mr. Harbin would stop talking about God and start telling me how to get over bulimia!

I gave him the diary I had been keeping for the past six weeks, thinking that if he read it he could figure out a way to help me get better. It was quite a few pages long by now, and I told him he could keep it until the following week if he would swear to take care of it and not let ANYONE read it.

"Molly, there's going to come a day when you won't be ashamed to talk about this. When you forgive yourself for your past mistakes and overcome your bulimia with God's help, you'll be able to help other people with the same problem," Mr. Harbin said as he leafed through my diary.

"He's crazier than I am!" I thought. "There's no way I'm going to tell anyone else about this." Then I said aloud, "I might get over this ... I hope so, but no one will ever find out. I couldn't stand it if anyone else knew about this."

Then Mr. Harbin gave me more suggestions for dealing with my emotions without turning to food. When the hour was almost over I was relieved that it was time to go.

Mr. Harbin smiled as I got up to leave, and he told me that he would be praying for me. He asked me if I would come back the following Friday.

We agreed on a time, and I left, my head spinning with new thoughts. Mr. Harbin was really a nice man, for someone who was religious, but I knew he was dead wrong about my being able to talk about bulimia and not be ashamed.

During the next few days the struggles over food continued as I spent countless hours trying to remember how I had gotten started on this vicious cycle of bingeing and purging. My mind was constantly running over my past life like an old movie.

Our family had been through some rough times during my childhood, but didn't everyone's family have ups and downs? I knew people who had been through a lot worse situations than I had, and they weren't bulimic. What ... or who ... could I blame my bulimia on?

My mom? No, heavens, no! Jane Smith had had a lot of trouble in her life, too, and had come through it. I loved her with all my heart. My father had been killed when I was just a baby, and Mom had been left all alone on the

West Coast while her family was in Ohio. She couldn't even drive a car! My brother, Bob, was only eleven months older than I. I shuddered as I remembered hearing how she had been left alone, thousands of miles from home, with two little babies. Surely that was worse than anything I had been through.

Later Mom moved back to Ohio and met and married Harold Smith, the only dad I ever knew. He was divorced and had two sons, my older step-brothers, Mike and Corky. Dad was always a good provider for the family and gave us all the things we needed.

When I was five years old my half-sister, Sara, was born with cystic fibrosis, a dreadful lung disease. Our family worked together to make Sara's short life as happy as possible. When she died at eight years old, as hard as it was on the family, we all made it through. Could I blame my bulimia on my sister's death? I could... but no, I was sure that I had brought this on myself.

Mom and Dad had tried to teach me the difference between right and wrong. Mom had taken me to Sunday school and taught me her beliefs and values, hoping that I would "turn out" good.

From all outward appearances I was a success. Now I had a dedicated, hard working husband, a lovely daughter and a great job at the post office. My parents loved me and were proud of me. I was sure I couldn't blame my bulimia on them.

No, the more I thought about it the more sure I was that the bulimia was my own fault. I had been very, very angry at fifteen when I was diagnosed as having diabetes. That was really when all this trouble had started.

I had begun losing weight around Christmas and had gotten worse in January. I was constantly thirsty and drank gallons of water a day. I made at least twenty-five trips to the bathroom every day and grew weaker and weaker as the days went by. Early in February Mom took me to the doctor and we found out the horrible diagnosis — DIABETES.

That's when my whole life changed. At first I dreaded getting up in the mornings. The disgusting job of testing my urine for sugar, followed by sticking a needle into my leg for insulin injections, was a lot for a fifteen-year-old to take.

But I think the thing that bothered me the most was the diet: No candy, no cookies, no milkshakes, no ice cream, NO! NO! NO! Oh, Mom baked me sugar-free cookies and desserts, but they really tasted pretty drab. I spent my whole life, it seemed, worrying about the injections, the diet, the urine testing and twice-weekly trips to the doctor's for blood tests.

During my senior year of high school I got a part time job in a bakery that was four blocks from our house. Mom had worked there decorating cakes for several years, and when the job opened up I jumped at the chance to earn my own money.

Mom had been concerned about my working there, afraid that I would yield to all the temptation of working in a bakery.

I told her not to worry; I was seventeen years old and capable of managing my diabetes. At first I was fine. I waited on customers in the front of the store, bagging up donuts, cookies, cakes and pies. After a while though, I figured it wouldn't hurt if I just tasted a little of the icing. Of course I tasted it when nobody was looking because everyone there knew I was a diabetic.

After a few days a taste became a whole cookie, a whole cupcake or a whole donut. I started taking more insulin to counteract the extra sugar I was putting into my body. It worked, too; my blood sugar tests were still pretty normal.

I was elated! I had gotten away with eating foods that had been banned to me for two years, and NOBODY knew. I continued this way, taking more insulin and sneaking around eating bakery goodies in secret, for a few months.

Then I realized I was gaining weight. I tried to get back on my diabetic diet, but somehow, now that I had gotten away with eating donuts, it seemed a shame to give it up.

I don't really remember the first time I made myself throw up. I don't even know what made me think of it. I do know that at first I only did it a couple of times a week. It became a private game to see how many things I could secretly eat and then throw up. I was thrilled to think that I was smart enough to work in the same place as my mom and get away with eating forbidden foods practically right under her nose without her knowing about it.

What started out as a game soon became a habit that I couldn't, or didn't want to break, bingeing and vomiting several times daily.

I got my weight back down to 125 and was pleased with my new appearance. I was able to eat as much as I wanted of anything that the bakery produced and not gain weight.

In August, 1977, I got a job as a nurse's aide in a nursing home. The bulimia continued to control me, and I felt superior to anyone who was heavier than I because I was able to eat what I wanted and still be thin.

I worked the eleven p.m. to seven a.m. shift at the nursing home. There were only two nurses and three other aides that I had to keep my secret activities hidden from, but it was harder to get my supply of binge food. The nursing home just didn't have the choices the bakery had. A prune juice and cracker binge wasn't nearly as fulfilling as donuts and cupcakes.

Luckily, — or so it seemed — soon after I started

working there a new-found friend showed me where the key to the big refrigerator in the main kitchen was kept hidden. Nobody was in the kitchen on the midnight shift, and there was a gold mine of food in there!

When my friend and I went to the kitchen together we would just take a few things for our 2:00 a.m. supper break. It was at other times during the night that I would sneak back and consume large amounts of food and go throw up without anyone catching me. There was such a bountiful supply of food there that I was sure that what I took would never be missed.

But soon I wasn't only taking the food at work — I began taking other things from other places — stores mostly. I just took little things: diet pills, laxatives, sleeping pills or anything small that would fit in my pocket or purse. I had to save my own money for my after-work binges.

I was trapped in a terrible circle of bingeing, vomiting, lying and stealing. I didn't even feel badly about it because nobody knew what I was doing.

After I had worked at the nursing home for a year, a girl named Diantha Saunders transferred from day to night shift. We became close friends, but I didn't tell her about any of my secret habits.

She told me about her older brother, Clyde, who had just gone through a divorce. She was always telling me how nice he was, and I knew that she could feel the pain her brother was going through.

Imagine my surprise when Diantha brought a Christmas card early in December for me from Clyde! It said that he had heard about me from Diantha and wondered if I would go out to lunch with him.

"What have I got to lose?" I thought. My romantic life was practically non-existent. I preferred to spend my free time alone with my favorite friend —food.

Why Am I Like This Anyway?   49

I agreed to the lunch date, but I was really nervous. This was the first blind date I had ever been on. When the doorbell rang I opened the door, and there stood a very handsome man. He had black hair and a mustache, big brown eyes and a beautiful smile. He was holding a bouquet of six red carnations!

We went to lunch and I found out that he really was as nice as Diantha had said. He had a daughter, Sherri, who was almost two and lived with her mother. He proudly showed me a picture of his little girl, a beautiful child who strikingly resembled her dad.

I had never believed in love at first sight before, but that afternoon I was in love. I kept looking at the flowers he had brought me and wondering if he would ever ask me out again.

Well, he did. We had wonderful times together, and when we couldn't be together we would talk for hours on the phone. During our courtship I didn't consciously try to stop the bingeing and purging; it just sort of slowed down. I had other things in my life now to occupy my mind. I still purged occasionally but not everyday.

On April 14, 1979, we were married. I had been working another part-time job, delivering mail for the Post Office, for about a year before I met Clyde. After Clyde and I got married I quit the nursing home job and was happy to work only on Saturdays.

In September of 1979 we bought our first home, a small two-bedroom with a great living room and a fireplace. Clyde worked the three to eleven shift, and again I turned to food to fill my lonely evenings. I always stayed up until Clyde came home from work, and now I had a perfect place to get rid of the binge evidence: the boxes and wrappers from all the food were easily burned in the fireplace.

In September of 1981, when I found out I was pregnant,

I was excited about becoming a mother. I still didn't feel any guilt about my bulimic habits. I had a lot of doctor's appointments because there were many complications and risks due to my diabetes. I tried to eat healthy foods and do all the prenatal health care suggestions. When I ate foods that weren't on my prescribed diet during my pregnancy I did throw up, but I don't think that I did it more than a few times.

Due to my diabetic (and unknown to the doctors, bulimic) condition I was hospitalized six weeks before my due date. I was classified "high-risk." I guess it was God's will that I be where someone capable could take care of me. I certainly wasn't capable of taking care of myself.

My medical complications made a cesarean delivery necessary, and Becky was born March 3, 1982. She was a tiny, beautiful bundle of joy to Clyde and me. I remember being so happy and thinking that now with this beautiful child to fill my hours, I wouldn't have time for my old bulimic habits.

I was faced with the usual confusion of first-time mothering, however, and before my six week post-natal check up came around I was right back into my secretive life — bingeing, vomiting, and stealing.

That was pretty much how I lived until August of 1984 when I was arrested for shoplifting. It was the most frightening experience of my life.

I had been feeling pretty sick and knew that my blood-sugar must be really high, so I went to a local drug store and took a small bottle of blood-sugar testing strips. I had become so used to stealing that I hardly even thought about it any more.

Although I pleaded with the store owner to let me go, he called the police. I could see my life going down the drain. If everyone found out, I would lose my job. (They

Why Am I Like This Anyway? 51

don't let criminals work for the Federal Government.) I knew my husband would take my daughter and leave me. I would have nothing left to live for if people found out about me.

I tearfully told the store owner that I was sorry, that I was a diabetic and was really sick. He didn't respond.

I told him that I had never, never stolen anything before, that we were poor and that my husband was laid off from his job. (They were all lies — I had just gotten paid from the Post Office and had over $400 in my purse.)

He wouldn't change his mind. The police came and wrote me up and told me I would be getting a letter with a court date in a few days.

I left the store in a stupor. Suicide — that was the only answer. I couldn't let Clyde know that I had been arrested. I couldn't stand it if he left me.

That was one of the few times I prayed. There was a church on my mail route and I drove there, sat on the steps and cried out to God. "Oh, Lord, I'm sorry. Please, please get me out of this. I promise I will never steal again."

Then I wrote the store owner a letter and told him that if he pressed charges I would never go to court; I would kill myself first. Luckily, he dropped the charges.

I never stole again after that. The experience of being arrested made me realize that I had too much to lose. My life continued in my bulimia, though. The bingeing, vomiting and lying never stopped. Yes, I knew for certain that this bulimia was my own fault. There was nobody to blame it on but me. How had I ended up with such a loving husband, a beautiful daughter, a good job and a nice home? I had even won a brand new car in a raffle earlier that year! Why was I so miserable when I had so many good things in my life? I certainly didn't deserve any of them.

Now here I was, trying so hard to stop these terrible sins. Since the day I had heard Cynthia Rowland on the radio it seemed as if my life was almost impossible to live. I wanted so badly to do what was right and continually ended up doing what was wrong.

Since I had told Clyde about my bulimia he had been treating me quite differently. Oh, I knew he still loved me, but I felt I was being watched every moment we were together. Now that he knew about my bulimia, I wasn't even allowed to lock the bathroom door. When I went in after supper and stayed too long, Clyde would come in to see what I was doing. I felt like a bad little girl who couldn't be trusted. I was able to keep from bingeing for a few days after seeing Mr. Harbin, but my mind was in constant turmoil. I couldn't even have a meaningful conversation with anyone because every thought was of food.

One of the articles in the NAAS newsletter had mentioned anti-depressant medications that doctors sometimes prescribed to treat bulimia. One of the girls at the support group had told me the name of something she was taking and said that it seemed to help. Since I was still having so much trouble with my self-defeating thoughts, I decided to call my family doctor and see if he would give me something. Wouldn't it be wonderful if I could take a pill to take away the pain of overcoming bulimia?

I called my family doctor and made an appointment for the week following my first session with Bud Harbin. When I confessed my years of bulimia to my doctor he was amazed.

He had begun treating me for diabetes a year after I graduated from high school when I had gotten my blood sugar so screwed up that I ended up in the hospital in a diabetic coma for a week. Of course he didn't know that the cause of it was bulimia, and after I was well again I just devised better ways to balance my insulin with my bingeing.

Since then I had experienced several severe insulin reactions resulting in seizures. I had binged and vomited, then taken more insulin to take care of what I couldn't throw up. I knew the seizures had scared Clyde to death. My body would stiffen, and I would grind my teeth together during the seizures. I always woke up with my tongue swollen and bleeding. My head would ache, and my muscles were sore for days afterwards. I never realized that the bulimia was the cause of my seizures. I guess I just thought that I'd have to be a better judge of how much insulin to take.

I nervously told my doctor the whole story and gave him the article about the medications that were used to treat bulimia. He gave me a prescription for a very low dosage of Imipramine, an anti-depressant, and encouraged me to continue seeing Bud Harbin and going to the support groups.

"You know it's a real miracle you're even alive, don't you?" he said. "I'm glad you finally decided to get help. It may take a while for you to see any change in how you feel when you start taking this...you might not see any improvement at all."

"I'm desperate," I said. "I'll give anything a try."

I had gone eleven days without bingeing and vomiting by my second appointment with Bud Harbin on August 22nd. I was worried about what he had thought when he read my diary. I knew he was a Christian, and I had used some words to describe myself and my bulimia that I was sure he wouldn't approve of.

To my surprise he didn't say anything about my language.

"You don't like yourself very well, do you?" he asked.

"Well...I don't know...I guess not," I really didn't

know how to answer that question.

"Molly, the Bible says 'love your neighbor as yourself.' Did you ever hear that?" He put great emphasis on the "as."

I nodded.

"What that means is this: to really love anyone else you have to love yourself first."

That was difficult for me to understand. Of course I loved Clyde, Becky, my friends and my family. What did that have to do with loving myself? There was not much here to love as far as I could see.

He was also concerned about what I was eating. I had recorded in my diary what I ate each day and totaled up the calories. I tried to keep my total under 1000. If I went over that I either vomited or felt like a failure. The really great days were when I could stay under 600 calories.

"It seems as if you eat at restaurants a lot. Too many salads... it doesn't sound like any diabetic diet that I've ever heard of." Mr. Harbin had already told me that he was hypoglycemic and had to follow a restricted diet similar to the one I was supposed to be following. "Do you think you might be able to eat healthier foods at home?"

"I'm afraid to have food in the house! When I go to the grocery store the same thing always happens — I buy the groceries and try to put them away without eating them. If I do get them put away I just walk around the house thinking about food. I bet it wouldn't be ten minutes after I got home before I'd be back in the kitchen eating everything. Then I'd have to throw up, and the food would be all gone anyway," I said, trying hard to make him understand. "If I go out and get a salad, I know that no matter how much lettuce I eat I won't get fat or want to throw up."

Then I gave him more excuses: "Clyde and Becky like to eat out; I work every day, and I'm too tired to fix

Why Am I Like This Anyway? 55

supper... eating out is a lot cheaper than buying a bag of groceries only to have it end up in the toilet. Besides that, I've been terrified of grocery stores since I've been trying to get over this."

Mr. Harbin suggested that I plan a meal and buy just what I needed for that meal and no more.

Plan a meal? Me? Right now that thought was absurd. Sure, I had cooked plenty of meals since I'd been married. I would start eating while supper was cooking, eat supper with Clyde and Becky, continue afterwards until there were no leftovers, then go throw up. It never failed.

He talked to me about praying before I went into the store. I really wanted to believe that God could help me do anything, but praying for strength to go to the store and buy groceries for a meal seemed a little on the crazy side.

After I left, I thought a lot about asking God to help me through the planning, buying groceries and preparing a meal. I wasn't very good at talking to God. The prayers that I had tried had never been answered. Would this be any different?

That evening Clyde and I talked a lot about what Mr. Harbin had said. Clyde encouraged me to try it and suggested that we have spaghetti. There was never anything in the house to eat anymore, and I felt that I was being unfair to him so I decided I would try.

I made a list before I went to the store and prayed that I would buy healthy foods. I bought the items on my list for the meal and a few other things — cereal, milk, cottage cheese, bread. Then I went over by the cookies.

"Just one package," I thought. "Clyde needs some cookies. It's not fair for him to be denied cookies just because of my stupid fears!"

Saturday, August 24 — I'm at home sitting in my

car. I just went in the house and started putting the groceries away. After I put everything away I got the cottage cheese back out and started eating right out of the carton.

"Stop! Stop!" I thought. "What are you doing?" So I put the lid back on and ran out here to the car. I could easily have eaten the whole thing. I ate three big bites before I stopped. I know if I had eaten the cottage cheese I would have had more. Toast, cereal, milk, cookies, more, more, more. Then I would have gone and vomited! Why can't I stop feeling this way? Do I really hate myself that much? Help me, LORD! I feel so strange! I wish Clyde were here — I need a hug real badly. My head is spinning. What's wrong with me? Please stop these feelings I have!

After writing this in my diary I shut my eyes and tried to clear my mind. After a few deep breaths I felt better. I went to Judy's house to pick Becky up, then came home and put three pieces of gum in my mouth so I wouldn't taste the food I was cooking for supper.

I had planned to make biscuits but decided that it would be safer to let Clyde and Becky have bread and butter with their spaghetti. I measured ½ cup of spaghetti for myself and had a big salad. I ate slowly and made it through the meal without much trouble.

After washing the dishes, I spied the cookies on top of the refrigerator. Clyde and Becky were watching T.V. so I reached up and took 2 cookies out and crammed one into my mouth. I stopped — What was I doing? I threw the other cookie in the trash and went to my bedroom and grabbed my diary.

Oh, I am so bad! Knock it off, Molly! You are a diabetic, remember? NO MORE COOKIES!

During the next few days the fight in my mind raged on. I had been taking the medication my doctor had given

Why Am I Like This Anyway? 57

me but could see little, if any, difference in the way I felt. I decided to call the hospital to see if they had any classes for newly diagnosed diabetics. I thought that if I could re-learn the diabetes management program I might have an easier time fighting the bulimia.

The Director of Education at the hospital informed me that the next series of classes wouldn't begin until November. When I explained the reason for my inquiry she suggested that I talk to the hospital dietician.

I went to the hospital and the dietician wanted me to tell her how I was eating at present.

That was easy to answer — one piece of dry toast for breakfast, an apple for lunch — then I would try to eat a normal meal for supper.

She shook her head and said, "No wonder you want to binge! How do you think your body can function when you don't put any food in it?"

She told me to think of my body like a car.

"They won't run without gas, oil and proper maintenance; it's the same with your body. It needs fuel to keep it functioning properly."

"I guess that makes sense," I said, shrugging my shoulders.

She explained in detail the 1200-calorie diabetic diet to me. It sounded impossible. If I ate all that food I would surely get fat!

She assured me that I wouldn't gain weight on a 1200-calorie diet. She sympathized with my plight: she had counseled diabetic women and bulimic women with their diets, but had never encountered someone with both problems before. She agreed that being diabetic was bad enough without having bulimic tendencies to deal with.

I thanked her and left her office clutching the list of foods that I could safely eat and promised myself once again to try my best to do better.

My step-father, Harold Smith, affectionately known as "Smittee" was employed at the Post Office in the maintenance department. In fact, Dad was the one who had helped me get my job at the Post Office in the first place. Some mornings when I got to work early I stopped by his office in the basement to shoot the breeze. Dad was always easy to talk to. We spent most of our morning visits discussing the activities of the various employees at the Post Office.

In the two months since my fight with bulimia began I had lost quite a bit of weight, and Dad was worried about me. He had expressed his concern before, and I had smiled and said that I was just trying to lose a few pounds.

But near the end of August I had rubbed a sore place on my tailbone that was bleeding, and I told my Dad about it one morning at the Post Office. I told him that I couldn't sit in the bathtub and that sitting in the car all day on the mail route was becoming more unbearable as the days went by.

"You'd better stop this dieting, Molly," Dad said with a worried frown. "You're really starting to look bad — your bones are sticking out!"

I shuddered at his statement and knew that he was right. The night before I had stood naked in front of the full-length mirror in our bedroom and studied my body, something that I could rarely bring myself to do. I could plainly count each rib, and my hip bones protruded as they never had before. I hated to admit it, but I WAS starting to look a bit on the unhealthy side.

I hadn't planned to let my parents know about my bulimia; I didn't want to burden them with my problems. After all, their responsibility for me had ended when I left home. But since it was obvious that I was losing too much weight, I decided that maybe it was time to let them know. So there in the Post Office basement I gathered up all my courage and told Dad some of the things that I had been going through in the past few weeks.

At first he seemed stunned by what I told him. He couldn't believe that I had been bingeing and forcing myself to throw up all these years without anyone's finding out. We didn't get into a long discussion about all that I had done during my bulimic years. Instead I gave him the book about Cynthia Rowland and, with it, the job of breaking the news to Mom. I thought that if they both read the book they might be able to better understand what was wrong with me. I made him promise to keep it a secret. I didn't want anyone at the Post Office to find out how disgusting I was.

That evening I told Clyde that I felt I should go to my parents' house and talk to them. There was no telling what they were thinking of me at this point in time. I wanted to assure them that I was doing all the things that were necessary for recovery, and that they had no reason to be worried, even though I wasn't completely sure that that was the case.

I went to Mom and Dad's and explained my struggle with bulimia as briefly as possible. I had expected them to be disappointed in me, but to my surprise they were very supportive. They were proud that I was doing so well (I may have stretched the truth a little on that point) and were glad that I had found a counselor who knew how to deal with bulimia. Telling my parents wasn't nearly as hard as I had thought it was going to be. I thanked them for taking it with such grace and promised them that I would try to stay on the diabetic diet and not lose any more weight.

As I left their house, I knew that I hadn't told them the whole truth . . . I knew that the struggle was far from being over. But at least the problem was out in the open now, and for that I was thankful.

PART II

WHO IS THIS JESUS I THOUGHT I KNEW?

4

Soul Searching

Tuesday, September 10, 1985 — I followed Susan into the restaurant, anxiously wondering if I would be able to eat a meal with another person who was bulimic. I had met Susan only two weeks before at the NAAS support group. As we stood in line waiting to order, the memory of our meeting flashed through the back of my mind. I winced as I remembered the scene I had made.

Judy hadn't been able to go with me so I had driven to the most recent support group meeting alone. It seemed like I was getting worse instead of better, and I had gone into the group with an angry, resentful attitude. Since my appointment with the dietician, I had become sick and tired of thinking about food all the time.

The conversation in the group had been centered around food. Terri and Tricia had tried to stress to the six of us that were present that there were no "bad" foods —that everything could be eaten in moderation as we learned to be responsible for our actions in recovery.

I had listened to the women discuss this food and that food until I could stand it no longer. In my frustration I had exploded into a tirade of complaints.

"How would you guys like to be diabetic? There are hundreds of things that I can't eat! Even if I ever do get over bulimia I'll never be able to eat donuts and ice cream! I can't! And how would you like to have to stick a needle in your leg twice a day just to stay alive? And count every single piece of food that goes into your mouth? See these little scars on the ends of my fingers? Four times a day I have to stick my fingers and squeeze a little drop of blood out to check my blood sugar! Not only that, but last week my husband hid the scales, and now I'm afraid to eat because I won't know how much I weigh! I know it's stupid, but it all makes me so darn mad!"

I had stopped and was horrified at myself for my outburst. Terri and Tricia tried to get me to talk more, but after I had apologized I remained quiet for the rest of the meeting.

After the meeting had ended Susan had invited me to meet her for supper before the next support group. I thought it was rather amazing since this was the first time I had ever seen her — especially after acting like such an idiot in the group.

Now here we were, getting ready to eat a meal together. We both ordered salads and sat down to eat. I picked up my fork and was ready to take a bite when I saw Susan bow her head in a silent prayer. I watched her with envy. She seemed so calm, not nervous like I was. I didn't know anything about this woman other than the fact that she was bulimic. Why in the world would she want to have supper with me?

As we began eating our meal we chatted about our lives, our families and our backgrounds. Susan was thirty-one years old, single and lived alone.

She had moved to Columbus from a small Ohio town and worked as a secretary for a large insurance firm.

When the conversation lapsed into an awkward silence Susan touched my hand and said quietly, "I've been praying for you since we met, Molly. You sounded so angry and upset last time."

"I know — I made a real fool of myself last time, didn't I?" I said, laughing. "You think they'll let me back in tonight?"

"Of course they will," she said with a smile. Then slowly her expression changed to a worried frown. "Listen . . . I don't want to stick my nose into your business... but I think I could help you, if you'd let me."

"Sure, I'll take any advice you're willing to give me — the stuff I'm doing now to try to stop doesn't seem to be working very well," I said, excited that she might be able to help me.

Susan began telling me the story of her life, her voice barely above a whisper. When she was a little girl, before she even started grade school, her father began to sexually abuse her. She told me that her concept of love was all wrong, that each time her father hurt her he told her he loved her. He told her not to cry and rewarded her with candy and praise in order to keep their "secret."

I felt myself becoming uncomfortable as she talked about her childhood, afraid that someone would hear. I couldn't imagine why on earth she was telling me about it.

Susan said that the sexual abuse had gone on for many years and that when she was fifteen years old she had started dealing with her frustration over her situation with bulimia.

"Didn't you ever tell anyone?" I whispered. I wondered how anyone could live through such a long ordeal.

"Not until many years later, Molly. I moved away from home when I was eighteen and tried to forget the past... but I was still bulimic. I never had any close friends — nobody I could tell about my past or my bulimia. About a year ago I read an article about bulimia in a magazine. It's weird, but I thought I was the only person who ever binged and then vomited. I thought that being thin was the only hang-up I had — but I had pushed all the terrible memories of what my father had done underneath the bulimia. I tried to forget it, but it was still there."

I reached over and squeezed her hand. I felt a huge lump in my throat, and as much as I wanted to offer her some comfort, I couldn't say anything.

"I don't want you to feel sorry for me, Molly," Susan said quickly. "Last week when you said what you did at the support group... Remember? About being mad that you were diabetic?"

"But what does that have to do with what happened to you?" I asked her, feeling a bit confused about this whole conversation.

"It's anger — anger at people who've hurt us, anger at circumstances beyond our control and anger at ourselves for our mistakes — that feeds the bulimia. When I read that article in that magazine it said something about unresolved childhood trauma that triggers bulimia. I thought that my bulimia was all my father's fault. I tried to stop bingeing and vomiting, but I couldn't. Then I got so angry that I went to him and slammed the magazine down on his desk. I pointed my finger at him and said, 'Read this! This is what's wrong with me! And it's all your fault! If I have to go to get treatment for this you're going to pay for it!' " Susan's voice began to tremble.

I was caught up in her anger and felt hate growing in me for this man that I didn't even know.

Susan continued, "I had kept all that anger inside me all those years. It grew and festered just like a sore, down in my subconscious. Then when it started coming out I didn't know what to do with it, so I handled it the only way I knew how — by lashing out at my father. In all my life I had never experienced anger — I didn't know how. Then I started seeing a Christian counselor who knew about adult victims of incest and bulimia. It was then that I REALLY accepted Christ as my Savior.

"Because He forgave me and loved me I was able to

work through my anger and forgive my father. I just feel sorry for him now . . . I pray that he will become a Christian and know the peace that I know."

"How could you forgive that? He deserves to go to hell for what he did!" I said angrily. "Do you actually think he could ever go to heaven after all the terrible things he did to you?"

Tears began to well up in Susan's eyes, and I knew I had hurt her with my angry outburst.

"We all deserve hell, Molly. None of us deserve heaven. That's why Jesus came to die for us." She stopped talking, and there was an uncomfortable silence. Neither of us had eaten much once she began telling me about her past.

I mumbled an apology and tried to eat more of my salad. Susan lifted a napkin to her cheek and wiped away her tears. "I'm sorry to be so emotional, Molly . . . The past can't be changed, and sometimes the memories are still painful. But the pain isn't for me — it's for my father. Maybe I shouldn't have told you all this . . . It's just that I ache to share with you the comfort I've known through Jesus . . . and with everyone else who struggles with bulimia."

I assured Susan that I admired her for her strength and courage. I had never known anyone with that kind of love for someone who had hurt her so badly.

Soon it was time for the support group to start. During the session I was glad that a couple of new women were doing most of the talking — my mind was obsessed with thoughts of my conversation with Susan. The peace that she seemed to have in spite of her bulimia was difficult for me to comprehend. Her life had been much more traumatic than mine, yet her attitude was one of praise. She wasn't completely free from the desire to binge and vomit and even had occasional slips, but she was sure of her future — freedom from bulimia. And she seemed so concerned about me. Why? I barely knew her, and yet she had reached out and shared a painful part of her past in an effort to help me.

When the group ended Susan gave me a hug. "Please call me if you need to talk. Call collect — God pays my phone bills," she said, smiling. "I really care about you... I'll be praying for you."

On the way home from Columbus my mind was in turmoil. I didn't know what I was feeling. How could Susan praise God when He had allowed such awful things to destroy her life? But was she destroyed? No, not at all. She was happy to be alive. Why couldn't I be like that?

I thought about Bud Harbin — he was a Christian. I thought I was, but I certainly didn't feel like one. I prayed day after day that God would take away the awful feelings and desires to binge and vomit. I didn't want anyone to find out about the bulimia, but everyone was finding out anyway. God must not be hearing my prayers. I still felt that I was being punished for all the lies I had told and the things I had stolen during my bulimic years.

When I got back to Mt. Vernon I drove up and down the streets looking for a place to get binge food. As I pulled into a grocery store parking lot Susan's words kept echoing in my brain. "I ache to share Jesus with you... I really care about you... I'll be praying for you."

How could Jesus forgive me for the past when I was sitting at the grocery store ready to do it again? I put my head down on the steering wheel, and tears began streaming down my face.

"Jesus, help me! Stop this evil desire I have. I don't want to be this way any more... please, please! I want to be like Susan. She's so happy and I'm so miserable... I don't want to do it again. I know it's wrong. I'm sorry for all the awful things I've done... Please, please help me!"

The bad Molly jumped up and down in my brain. "NO! NO! Do you think God could help you? He doesn't care about you! You're hungry, aren't you? Go on in the store and get some food!"

I wiped my tears away, went into the store and headed straight for the bakery department. Since it was late they had bagged up the leftover donuts and marked them half price. I picked up three of the bags and got a quart of chocolate milk. I got into my car and looked around to see if anyone was watching before I began cramming the donuts in my mouth. By the time I arrived at a nearby park, I had finished the donuts and the milk. There had been six donuts in each bag — eighteen all together. I looked around the park to make sure nobody was there. It looked safe, so I got out of the car, went behind some big bushes and stuck my fingers down my throat.

There was a sickening sweet taste in my mouth when I got home, and I hurried to brush my teeth. The clock said 11:00 when I finally crawled into bed beside Clyde. He gave me a kiss and a sleepy hug, then rolled over and went back to sleep.

I lay there and tried to forget what I had just done. I wanted to cry, but the tears would not come. This day had been a total disaster. I had gone twenty-six days without throwing up — almost a month! Now I'd have to start all over again.

What would Clyde think if he knew what I had just done? And Susan? And Judy? And Mr. Harbin? I decided not to tell anyone — not yet, anyway.

I wrote another hate letter to myself in my diary the next day and promised myself in big letters that I was "NOT GOING TO BINGE AGAIN."

On Friday, September 13 I had an appointment with Bud Harbin at the Nazarene College. Since fall quarter had begun I had to go there instead of to his home. I walked across the campus wondering if any of these smiling students were bulimic. Bud said he had counseled bulimic girls at the college — where were they? I felt I must be the only one in my hometown who had this problem.

I walked into Bud's office and told his secretary my name, wondering if she knew why I was here. In a few minutes Bud opened the door and smiled at me as I went in and sat down in his small office. Still smiling, he asked me how I had gotten along during the week.

Tears began to cloud my vision as I told him all about Susan and what I had done Tuesday night. This was the first time I had purged since I had started seeing him. I hated the fact that I had gone twenty-six days and then blown it all in one evening.

"Twenty-six days ... that's a long time," Bud said slowly. "Much better than several times a day, don't you think? You've been bulimic for an awfully long time — you can't expect to be cured overnight, can you? I personally think you've done remarkably well."

I smiled in spite of my anger over my recent failure. I guess he was right. He seemed to have a positive answer for every negative thing I said.

Bud wanted me to try to figure out what I had been feeling before I started to binge. "Who were you angry at? Susan?" he asked.

"NO! I wasn't angry at Susan. She was sweet and caring. I think when she told me about her past it made me jealous because she was so happy in spite of it all."

He leaned back in his chair and put his hands behind his head. "Why do you think she's happy, Molly? Do you think her faith in Jesus has anything to do with it?"

I sat silently for a minute or two. "Yes, I'm sure it does... How do you get that kind of faith, though? I try to remember to pray and think about Jesus, but I end up thinking about food. Then I hate myself for that."

Bud didn't answer for a moment, and when I looked up at him he was still sitting there studying me intently with his hands behind his head.

"You hate yourself... you're angry with yourself... you think you're no good. There must be something that you are still angry about, Molly." He was talking slowly. I could feel him staring at me as if he were trying to see into my soul.

"You said that Susan told you about her past because of something you said at the support group. Tell me about that."

I tried to recount what had happened as best I could. Yes, I had been angry about being diabetic and bulimic. Yes, I had displayed an emotion at the group that I rarely, if ever, displayed. But I was over that now. I firmly told Bud that I was definitely not angry about being diabetic now. I was just sick of thinking about food all the time.

"Did you ever read about Jesus' temptation by Satan in the desert? Jesus said, 'Man does not live by bread alone, but by every word that proceeds out of the mouth of God,'" Bud said. "Are you feeding your mind? You need spiritual food to grow spiritually. Bible reading and fellowship with other Christians, along with prayer, I believe, are necessary for real fellowship with God. Have you been to church since we started talking?"

"Here he goes again," I thought, "talking about church." I shook my head.

"Think about going, Molly. It couldn't hurt, could it?" Bud was smiling at me now. If only it were that simple.

Before I left, Bud told me about a girl at the college who was bulimic. He said that he had told her about the NAAS support group, and he wondered if I would allow her to ride to Columbus with me.

I said that I didn't mind — even though I wasn't

exactly thrilled about the prospect of admitting that I was bulimic to yet another resident of my home town. How many people were going to find out about this before I could recover?

Bud arranged for the girl to come to my house the following Monday so that we could get acquainted before the next night's support group.

She arrived right on time. She was tall and very beautiful. She wore pretty clothes and had immaculate blonde hair. And she was MUCH thinner than I. Her name was Ann.

I invited her in, and at first I felt mousy and awkward. Soon, though, we were both talking and nervously telling one another about our struggles. She was as frightened about coming to my house as I was about having her.

Ann was nineteen years old and had been anorexic before she became bulimic. As beautiful as she was, she felt terrible about herself — like me. I couldn't understand it — she was beautiful! I guess when you're bulimic it doesn't matter what you look like, you still feel terrible about yourself.

Tuesday, September 24 — My new friend, Ann, and I went to Columbus to the support group tonight and talked all the way there and all the way back. I feel like we are sisters. She was shy at the group because she'd never been there before, but she talked a little bit and said she wants to go again. God, bless Ann and me. Help us sort out our feelings and find an answer to our problems. Please help Ann feel better about herself. Thank you, Lord, for Ann. Guide me in my eating and in all areas of my life
—Molly.

I was glad that Ann was able to go with me, but one thing bothered me. Susan wasn't there. In a way I was glad because I didn't want to tell her what I had done after I had left the group the last time. I wondered if something had happened to her. I decided to try to call her later in the week.

Because of my preoccupation with food and struggling with bulimia, I was beginning to get in trouble at work. People on the mail route were calling in and complaining about my leaving them the wrong mail. Each time the postmaster called me in her office, I promised to do better, knowing that my job could be in jeopardy if I didn't shape up.

I was ready to leave the post office on Saturday, September 28, when another complaint came in. It hadn't been a week since I'd made the SAME mistake with the SAME customer. After another stern warning from the postmaster and a humbling apology from me, I left for the route.

"Pay attention, you jerk," I told myself. "You'll lose your job if you don't knock it off."

I was on the second street of my route when I noticed a flag on a familiar mailbox was up. This lady *always* had her flag up. Sometimes it was to mail letters, but many times she left me newsy notes and invited me to church. As I pulled up to her box, I hoped she just had letters to mail. But no — it was another note!

"Dear Molly, please come to church this Sunday. We have a new minister. He's really nice. Revival is next week."

I stopped reading and shut my eyes. God, why doesn't she leave me alone? I have enough trouble in my life right now without being bothered with going to church. I threw the note on the dashboard and continued on the route, trying to block every thought but that of delivering the mail out of my troubled mind.

That evening I talked to Clyde about going to church. I showed him the note from the lady on the mail route. He looked at it with disinterest so I decided not to pursue the idea. Besides, gnawing at the back of my brain I had a bad memory about a church we had attended.

At the church where I had been baptized, Clyde and I had attended Sunday school — in spurts. For a couple of months we would go every week; then we would slack off, deciding that there were more important ways we could spend our Sundays. Then we would think about Becky and make another half-hearted attempt at Sunday school for her sake.

After a prolonged period of Sunday school abstinence some now-forgotten circumstance resulted in Becky's and my going to Sunday school alone. There was a new couple in our young adults' class that I didn't particularly like. I had never seen them before, and all of a sudden this man was the teacher of the class. I didn't even know this couple's names. I just knew I didn't like them. The man was tall and good-looking; the wife was beautiful and perfect. They both knew a lot about the Bible — I thought they probably had the whole thing memorized. I had gotten into a slight argument with this lady and left the class in tears, vowing that I would never go back.

Now, almost a year later, I felt drawn to go back to church, partly because of Susan and Bud, who both seemed to think that living for Jesus was the only way to live, and partly out of curiosity. The lady on the mail route had said that there was a new minister at church, and she *had* invited me to go.

But what if I ran into that couple from Sunday school class? I didn't think I could face them, especially the woman.

After more deliberation I decided that if I had a free evening the next week I would try to go to the revival. It was a week when they would have church services every night. It couldn't hurt to go and meet this new minister. "Who knows?" I thought to myself. "If there is a slim chance that going to church will help the struggle I am having with bulimia, I might as well give it a try."

5

Glimmer of Hope

Tuesday, October 1 — All day long my nerves were on edge and I couldn't seem to do anything right. It was the wrong Tuesday for my support group meeting and I missed my new friends in Columbus terribly. The support group and my appointments with Bud Harbin were about the only things that kept me going. I tried to call my friends, Ann at the Nazarene College and Susan from the support group, but got no answer on either attempt. I felt an urgent need to talk to someone who knew what I was going through.

After racking my brain trying to think of something to do to get me out of the house, I remembered the invitation to our church's revival for this week. That would probably be better than staying at home and risking another binge.

After another tense meal that night I asked Clyde to go with me to the revival. "Please, I want to go, but I don't want to go by myself," I pleaded. "C'mon... it's only an hour long."

Clyde listened for a while to my reasons for wanting him to go and finally gave in, admitting that he was a bit curious about this new preacher, too.

The new preacher got up at the beginning of the service and introduced himself. I guessed him to be in his late twenties. He had dark brown hair, a mustache, glasses, and somehow he was able to keep a huge smile on his face all the while he was talking. His name was Pat

Hall. He and his wife, Debbie, and two small daughters, Shauna and Lindsey, had travelled to Mt. Vernon from somewhere in Georgia and had only been at Central Church of Christ for about two weeks. After his introduction he led those of us in attendance in a couple of songs.

As we were singing, I noticed that on the other side of the sanctuary sat the man and woman I had argued with in Sunday School many months before. I secretly hoped that when the revival service was over I could get out of there without having to face them.

The evangelist's message was about people who loved Jesus in spite of difficult circumstances. He told about a place where he had stayed in India where the people walked for miles to church, praising Jesus every step of the way. He talked about a man who had been paralyzed in a diving accident but was full of joy and living for Jesus. He told of a woman who had been abused for years in a concentration camp, and through Jesus' love was able to forgive and pray for those people who had mistreated her so terribly.

"What about you?" he said softly near the end of the service. "Jesus said, 'Come unto me all ye that labour and are heavy laden, and I will give you rest.' Won't you come and give your life to him as we sing . . ."

During the closing prayer, I shut my eyes tight and prayed the same prayer that I prayed almost every day.

"God, I'm sorry for being so bad. Please, please stop this bulimia. I hate it. I don't want to be this way. I just want to be normal."

On the way out, a few people talked to us, smiling and happy to see us. The very man and woman that I had been trying to avoid came over and began talking to us. The man shook Clyde's hand and said, "Hi, my name's

Mike Smith, and this is my wife, Ellen. Glad you could make it."

His wife smiled sweetly, and as I forced a smile and shook their hands I thought, "Sure, I bet you are."

Clyde and I turned to leave, and on the way out Pat Hall, the new preacher, shook Clyde's hand. As he was shaking my hand he said, "Are you members here?"

The question caught me off-guard. Were we?

"We come here once in a while," I said nervously as I felt that familiar panic rising in me. I had to get out of there...

"It was nice to meet you," I heard Clyde say to him as I quickly headed for the door.

On the way home Clyde said that he had enjoyed the service and thought that Pat Hall seemed like a pretty nice guy. I wasn't sure how I felt about him; I'd have to think it over.

Thursday, October 3 — I thought about many things today. About God, food and prayer. We used to say grace once in a while, but now I never think about it. I try to keep my mind straight and eat real slow, but when I just eat like I used to, I eat real fast. "Stuff it in, Molly! See how much you can eat, Molly! Go ahead, you can throw up!"

If I could stop and pray, maybe I could have better control. Something like this: Thank you, Lord, for this gift of food. Please help me eat moderately and wisely. Help me through this meal and the rest of this day. Amen.

If only that would slow me down and make me think.

That Sunday, Clyde agreed to go to Sunday school with Becky and me. I took Becky to her class in the basement and went to join Clyde in the young adults' class upstairs. There were about ten people there, and half of them were unfamiliar to me.

Mike Smith began to speak, and about ten minutes into the lesson the door opened. In walked Pat Hall, with a sheepish grin and a mumbled apology for being late.

I wasn't paying too much attention until someone made a comment about struggling with doing things that they knew were wrong.

"Even Paul had that," Pat said. He flipped though the pages of the Living Bible and began reading Romans 7:18: "I know I am rotten through and through so far as my old sinful nature is concerned. No matter which way I turn I can't make myself do right. I want to, but I can't. When I want to do good, I don't; and when I try not to do wrong, I do it anyway. Now if I am doing what I don't want to, it is plain where the trouble is: sin still has me in its evil grasp. It seems to be a fact of life that when I want to do what is right, I inevitably do what is wrong. I love to do God's will so far as my new nature is concerned; but there is something else deep within me, in my lower nature, that is at war with my mind and wins the fight and makes me a slave to the sin that is still within me. In my mind I want to be God's willing servant but instead I find myself still enslaved to sin. So you see how it is: my new life tells me to do right, but the old nature that is still inside me loves to sin. Oh, what a terrible predicament I'm in! Who will free me from my slavery to this deadly lower nature? Thank God! It has been done by Jesus Christ our Lord. He has set me free."

As Pat read the scripture I sat bolt-upright in my chair. What he was reading could have been written by me, except for the part about being set free.

As soon as Sunday school was over, I was more than ready to leave. I felt like a foreigner with these people and wanted to get out of that situation as soon as possible.

Glimmer of Hope   81

The rest of the day I kept thinking about what Pat had said. I didn't know very much about this Paul from the Bible, but from the conversation in class I had picked up a few bits of information. He was a man who had started out persecuting Christians and had ended up witnessing for Christ and writing a lot of the New Testament.

Tuesday, October 8, I got a letter from the church, a ballot for the election of elders and deacons. Most of the names on the page were unfamiliar to me, and I had no intention of voting, but I decided that it might be a good excuse to go and talk to Pat Hall. I could take the ballot back and tell him why I wasn't voting. Maybe I could tell him about my bulimia . . . Maybe he could help. I didn't even know him, so if he rejected me or thought I was disgusting it wouldn't matter. I just wouldn't go back.

The next day I drove to the church after I got off work and saw that his white Toyota was the only car in the parking lot, so I knew that he was alone. I went into the building and knocked timidly on his office door.

"Come in," he called out. When he saw me, he smiled and said, "Hi, Molly!"

I smiled back and was impressed that he remembered my name. I went in and nervously sat on the edge of the chair. I got the ballot out of my purse and explained that I didn't feel qualified to vote since I didn't know half of the names on the list.

"You don't have to vote," he said as he reached across his desk and took the ballot from me. "I *would* like to see more of you and Clyde at church though. You ought to get to know the people here. I haven't been here very long myself, but they all seem really nice . . . but let's don't talk about them. Tell me a little bit about yourself."

Before I knew it I found myself telling this total stranger all about my bulimia. Going into great detail, I described all the techniques I had used when I was constantly bingeing and purging. I explained my fears about coming to church because I felt like everyone there was better than I.

Pat had never heard of bulimia, so I gave him the newsletters from the Columbus support group that I carried in my purse.

I had been crying off and on during our conversation and after realizing that I was making a total fool of myself I got up to leave.

"I really don't know why I've told you all of this... you must really think I'm crazy," I said, shaking my head. "Don't tell anyone about this, O.K? If anyone here knew about me, I wouldn't be able to face them."

"Can I give you a hug, Molly? I think you need one," Pat said as he got up from his desk. He warmly enfolded me in his arms, and I felt that his concern for me was real and genuine. "Can I show these newsletters to Debbie? I think you need a friend in the church." I nodded.

"Before you go I want you to read something." He picked up a Bible from his desk and opened it, thumbing through the pages. "Philippians... here, read the third chapter, verses 12 through 14."

He held out his open Bible to me. My eyes focused on the verses and I silently read: "Not that I have already obtained all this, or have already been made perfect, but I press on to take hold of that for which Christ Jesus took hold of me. Brothers, I do not consider myself yet to have taken hold of it. But one thing I do: Forgetting what is behind and straining toward what is ahead, I press on toward the goal to win the prize for which God has called me heavenward in Christ Jesus" (NIV).

"Look at it this way," Pat said. "You're a lot better than you were four or five months ago, right? And now you have TWO new friends — Debbie and me. I'm glad you came in here to talk to me today. Any time you need a

Glimmer of Hope 83

shoulder to cry on, just come on in ... It's O.K. with me!"

I left Pat's office with a smile on my face and a spring in my step. Here I had "spilled my guts" to him, and he had given ME a hug! Amazing!

I went to my car and closed my eyes. "God, take my life, as ugly as it is. I hear that you forgive sins ... Jesus, you died for me, didn't you? Whatever it is that Susan, Bud Harbin and Pat Hall have ... whatever makes them able to love someone like me ... please give me what they have. Please, Jesus, take away the hate that I have for myself. Help me to love myself ... let me feel your love." I said the words out loud. They sounded strange to my ears, as if they were the words of someone else. I wondered if God had really heard me. But in that moment, I began to believe that God really could help me.

On Tuesday, October 15, Pat and Debbie had an open house party at their home for the members of the church. When Clyde and I arrived, Pat invited us in and told me that Debbie was in the kitchen. Then he and Clyde went into the living room to join some people who were gathered there.

I went into the kitchen to look for Debbie and the first thing I saw was a table heavily laden with all kinds of food. There were three of the church women standing by the sink, talking to Debbie.

When they saw me they all smiled and said, "Hi." I felt the familiar anxiety rising over me. My two worst fears — food and church people — were right here staring me in the face.

Debbie left the group, came right over to me and gave me a long hug.

I made lots of raw vegetables, and I got some Diet Coke for you," she whispered in my ear. "Are you O.K.?"

"Thanks," I whispered back. "Don't worry, I'll be fine." I was surprised by her caring display of affection.

After that the evening went pretty smoothly. I calmed down when I got out of the kitchen and rejoined Clyde in the living room. I smiled at the thought of a preacher's wife giving me a hug. I wished that we could be close friends, but I had to be realistic. She probably had too much to do to be friends with me.

That night when I went to bed, I looked back over the evening and felt a strange sort of contented peace. Several of the people that I had known slightly for years had talked to me as if they were really glad I was there. My life seemed to be going in the right direction at last.

For the next few weeks I tried hard to follow my prescribed diet. A few times I binged, but I refused to make myself throw up. I was still scared of being around food and afraid that anyone would find out about my bulimia, but I was excited about my new friends. I frequently called them on the phone, drove to the church to talk to Pat or stopped by their home to talk to Debbie, confident that whatever I told them would go no further. Debbie adopted me as her "sister" and their daughters, four-year-old Lindsey and five-year-old Shauna, began calling me "Aunt Molly."

I also continued my weekly appointments with Bud Harbin and twice monthly made the trip to Columbus to see my friends at the support group. I happily told everyone who knew about my bulimia when November 10 came, and I celebrated two months of freedom from my old habit of bingeing and purging.

On November 18 I went to the Halls' home when I was finished with work, and Shauna and Lindsey told me that they were in the basement working on some project. I went down and as soon as Debbie saw me she stopped what she was doing and gave me a hug.

"Go upstairs and get them, Pat," Debbie said.

Pat grinned and immediately bounded up the steps.

"Where's he going?" I asked, puzzled by his sudden departure.

"You'll see," Debbie answered with a smile.

In less than a minute Pat returned with his hands behind his back.

"All right. What's going on?" I said.

Debbie went over and stood close to Pat. I could see him handing her something behind their backs.

"Surprise!" Debbie said, and presented to me a small bean-bag doll with the words "Peanut Butter" printed on its tiny T-shirt. Recently I had jokingly told her that there was a ten-foot jar of peanut butter in my kitchen that I was afraid to be alone with.

"I dare you to binge on peanut butter with this sitting on top of the jar."

Before I could thank her Pat said, "Wait. That's not all."

He handed me a business-size envelope with my name typed on it.

I opened the envelope, carefully took out the typed page and began to read it. I couldn't believe my eyes! It was a lengthy contract!

In the contract I was to promise to stay on my diet from the hospital and "not go crazy or freak out" if I happened to eat something that wasn't on my diet. Also, it said that I was to call or visit Pat or Debbie anytime, day or night, if I saw problems developing with my bulimia. I laughed as I noticed that he had spelled it BULEMIA.

Pat had a section of things in the contract that he said he needed to work on, too. Among them was to spend more time on his sermons and to stay on a regular exercise routine.

The contract was to remain binding until January 2, 1986, or until we died, whichever came first. Pat explained that the purpose of that particular date was to get me through the holidays that were right around the corner.

Finally, we were both to promise to "seek the guidance and strength of God Almighty to help us because we can do all things through Christ, who strengthens us."

I didn't know whether to laugh or cry. I looked up from the contract to see Pat and Debbie grinning at me from ear to ear.

"I . . . I don't know what to say," I said, my voice trembling. "I love you guys."

I went to them and put my arms around both of them at the same time. I couldn't speak for a few minutes because I was choked up with emotion, and tears were running down my cheeks. I didn't deserve the unbelievable love that these two special people were pouring out on me.

6

Holiday Encounters

Getting involved in church activities definitely had its ups and downs. Clyde and I had made a few friends in the body of believers at Central Church of Christ, but there was still a certain couple there that made me uncomfortable, to say the least. It was Mike and Ellen Smith, the adult class Sunday school teacher and his wife. Ellen and I still had a barrier between us from that long-ago disgreement in Sunday school. I wasn't sure if she even remembered it — but I sure did.

I had talked to Pat about the matter before, putting this new minister in the uncomfortable position of trying to bridge a gap between two of the "flock."

"Mike and Ellen really are nice. If you got to know them you'd probably end up liking them," Pat said to me one afternoon. "Who knows? Maybe you and Ellen could be good friends."

"Sure, when pigs fly!" I told him. There was no way I could ever be friends with the two of them.

The Thanksgiving holiday was drawing near, and the church had planned a carry-in dinner for Saturday, November twenty-third. Clyde and I both wanted to go, but I had a terrible feeling of dread. There would be lots of people and TONS of food there. That morning's diary entry said this:

> Help me, O Lord. Lead me not into temptation, but deliver me from evil. Cookies, cakes, pies and

brownies are everywhere. The devil wants me to go back to my old, evil ways.

That night we went to the basement of the church, and I was fine as long as I stayed away from the long tables full of food. Mike and Ellen were busy talking to some people on the other side of the basement, and there was a big enough crowd there that I didn't have to face them.

Debbie came over to me and held my hand while Pat said the prayer.

"Thank you, Lord, for Pat and Debbie," I prayed silently. "And please, please let me get through this meal without going crazy."

Someone came over and began talking to Debbie, so Clyde tracked Becky down and we took a place in the serve-yourself food line.

I carefully selected my meal: raw vegetables and a small piece of turkey. Becky went and sat at a short table that was set up for the little kids, and Clyde and I sat at the end of an empty table.

The tables were beginning to fill up, and I looked up in despair as I noticed Mike and Ellen Smith heading for the two empty seats across the table from Clyde and me.

"Oh, God! Why did I come?" I thought. Immediately I was overwhelmed with a feeling just short of terror. "I knew I should have stayed home!"

After asking if we were saving those seats for anyone, they sat down. My panic slowly began to subside as Mike and Clyde began to talk about their jobs.

Ellen made a comment about how cute Becky was in the dress she was wearing, and our conversation soon turned to the subject of having babies. Ellen was pregnant and hoping for a girl, since they already had two boys.

Things were going pretty smoothly, and I found myself almost enjoying the conversation until Clyde, Mike and Ellen went back to the tables for dessert. The three of them came back with their plates filled with samples of the cakes, cookies, pies and brownies that people had brought.

"Oh, I know I shouldn't be eating this, but... well, I *AM* eating for two," Ellen said, laughing.

I wanted to stand up and scream, "GET AWAY FROM ME WITH THAT FOOD!!" Instead I said I was going to the restroom and snuck up the stairs to the darkened Sunday school room.

I was angry with myself for my stupid, irrational fears. No one at church except Pat and Debbie knew about my problem. I knew it was normal for people to eat dessert after meals. It wasn't their fault that I couldn't handle being around food. I asked God to calm me down and give me strength; then I went back downstairs. By this time the tables had been cleared of the plates and remaining food, and I hurried to rejoin Clyde, Mike and Ellen.

Pat got his guitar out and called everyone to join in singing. We sang slow, sweet songs of thanksgiving and praise. During the singing I looked at Ellen, her smiling face aglow with joy. Was it because of the expectancy of her unborn child? Or was it her love for the Lord? I hated to admit it, but Ellen really was pretty nice. Mike wasn't so bad, either. I looked back over the evening and was thankful that I had come.

That night I wrote a short note to Mike and Ellen. I told them that I was glad that they had sat with us and that we had enjoyed the time we had spent with them at the Thanksgiving supper. Maybe someday we would be friends; who could tell?

It was my usual custom to take the week of Thanksgiving off from work and get Christmas shopping taken care of. This year, though, I was afraid of any unstructured time that might leave me an option to binge. I began Monday morning with five sheets of paper, and on each one I made a list of things to do that particular day.

During one of my numerous shopping trips that week, I bought myself a gift — a more modern translation of the Bible. It was much easier for me to understand than the King James Bible I had gotten for graduation. I had never read much of this mysterious book, but I firmly believed that it was the Word of God and that He had it written for a very important purpose — to be read and studied by His children.

Thanksgiving Day came and we went to Clyde's parents' house for the meal. Clyde has two brothers and four sisters and lots of nieces and nephews, so the house was full of people. I focused my thoughts on how good things had gone in my life lately; it was over two months now since I had binged and purged. The day dragged on and on, but I ate a sensible meal and left my in-laws' house feeling rather satisfied with myself.

Thanksgiving Day, November 28 — Never have I known so many things to be thankful for: My Bible — to be able to read Your Word. Eyes to see the wonders You have made. Hands to touch others. Arms to give and receive hugs. I thank You, Lord, because I am fearfully and wonderfully made. I am very sorry for the years of abuse I have done to myself. Please, God, give me rest, for my brain is having fights again. The bad Molly says, "Eat! Eat! Eat!" and I know I've had enough. Please help me to honor the contract given to me by Pat. Thank You for Your care and for Your Son, Jesus. Amen.

A week after Thanksgiving something happened that

really puzzled me. Bud had told me not to condemn myself if I had a setback, but to look at the circumstances surrounding it and try to figure out what caused it. The other times that I had binged were always preceded by some emotional upheaval of stress, anxiety or pain.

I began December 5 with praise in my heart and on my lips. It had been over ten weeks since I had binged and I was sure I was totally recovered from my bulimia. Clyde had been coming to church with me, and we had been communicating with more openness and honesty than ever before. I sang all that day on the mail route. The sun was shining, the sky was blue, God was in His heaven, and all was right with the world. I was happier that day than I could ever remember being.

That evening the bad Molly, as if lying dormant for all those weeks, rose up in her evil ugliness. After lying to Clyde about where I was going, I left the house and drove from one fast food place to another in the worst binge I had been on in months. It didn't make sense — I HAD BEEN HAPPY ALL DAY LONG!

I didn't tell Clyde, but the next afternoon I went to the church to talk to Pat. I couldn't look him in the face as I told him what I had done. The contract was broken ... and so was my heart.

After giving me a hug, Pat assured me that he wasn't angry at all and that he had something to admit to me.

"You've kept the contract longer than I have," he said. "I haven't done my exercises; I've been late coming to the office, and have you noticed? My sermons have been pretty sloppy lately."

I laughed and told him that I hadn't noticed. He was sure good about knowing what to say to make me feel better.

At the support group I hesitated to tell of my setback because some of the women there looked up to me in light of my apparent success.

My good friend Susan had been having a rough time, too. She had experienced a couple of binge-purge episodes since the last time we had met.

"I can see how I was taking my freedom from bulimia for granted," Susan said. "I wasn't relying on God's strength and wisdom, but slipping back into an 'I can solve all my own problems' attitude. We all have setbacks, but we just have to get up and try again. Don't be so hard on yourself. Remember, we're here for support. After all — this IS a support group!"

She was right. I smiled, and my heart filled with love for Susan. Her love and her testimony had given me a desire to try to find out what God wanted for my life.

During the two weeks prior to Christmas I binged and purged several times. I had lost my ten-week cushion of time, and when I felt the urge to binge I guess it didn't seem so important to fight it.

What was happening to me? Had I given up? Was it easier to just give in to the Bad Molly that I formerly thought I had conquered? I couldn't seem to get 'back on the wagon,' and I once again experienced feelings of self-hate because of my failures.

Then I figured out why I was slipping back into my old bad habits — or so I thought. I needed to be punished — that was the answer. When children do what's wrong, you punish them because you love them and want them to do what's right ... for their own good, right? I KNEW the difference between right and wrong, and I continued to do wrong. It was my choice. If anyone really loved me, then they should love me enough to punish me, so I would stop bingeing and vomiting.

I wrote Pat a long, crazy letter telling him that I wished someone would hit me. After all, I deserved it, didn't I? I even found a scripture in my Bible that fit perfectly:

Psalm 141:3, 5 — *Set a guard over my mouth, O Lord; keep watch over the door of my lips. Let a righteous man strike me — it is a kindness; let him rebuke me — it is oil on my head. My head will not refuse it.*

The next time I went to talk to Pat, he was different than I had ever seen him before. I could tell he was disgusted with me.

"I can't change you, Molly," he said with a note of anger in his voice. "And I won't hit you. What do you want me to say? You don't call me before you binge; you only call me after you've done it and then you start crying around about how bad you are. I CAN'T change you. The only one who can do that is YOU."

He wouldn't physically hit me, but the words he had just said felt like a slap in the face. Blinking back tears, I left his office without saying good-bye.

After an hour or two of being thoroughly depressed, I realized that he was right. I was always trying to pawn the responsibility for my recovery on someone else. I wanted someone to MAKE me do better. Feeling once again like a jerk, I called Pat and Debbie's home to apologize, but Pat wasn't there. Debbie told me that they had been having some problems in their marriage. She said that he was always gone and that he paid more attention to the people at church than he did to her.

This couldn't be happening! Preachers are supposed to have good, happy marriages. I loved Pat and Debbie with all my heart, and one of the things that I wanted most in the world was for them to be happy.

I was sure that the problems they were having were all my fault. The reason they never had any time alone was because I was always hanging around, monopolizing all their time. I needed to stop feeling sorry for myself and see what I could do to make up for the damage I had done to their marriage. I wrote them a letter, pouring my heart out in concern for them and apologizing for whatever role I had played in causing this turmoil in their marriage. I promised them that I wouldn't bother them again with my problems and that I hoped we could still be friends.

Well, now I was definitely in a pickle. I felt that I had nobody to talk to. I didn't feel that I could burden Clyde, Pat or Debbie anymore; the Nazarene College was closed until January so I couldn't talk to Bud, and the support group had been called off because the second Tuesday fell on Christmas Eve. What was I going to do now?

I tried to examine the changes occurring in my life the past few weeks that could be causing me to return to my bulimic behavior. I was back, for the time being, to being my own therapist.

Even though he was only twenty-nine years old, my brother, Bob, was in the hospital because of severe heart problems and trouble with his back. His wife, Diantha, was Clyde's younger sister. We were all worried and upset by his condition, especially at this time of the year.

When he had become a Christian at seventeen he had been very devoted to the work of the church but had fallen away because of one thing or another. Now that he was in serious trouble, I prayed that he would remember the real source of comfort — Jesus Christ.

Even though Pat barely knew my brother, as a favor to me he accompanied me to the hospital to stay with Diantha on December 23 while Bob had surgery on his back. The surgery was successful, but because of his heart condition, Bob had to stay in intensive care. Pat and I left Diantha at the hospital after the doctor assured us that Bob was out of danger.

On the hour-long drive home from the hospital, Pat and I were able to talk like old friends. After we both had apologized for our various grievances toward each other, I tried to give Pat advice about working out his problems with Debbie. He told me firmly that they had ALMOST worked things out and for me not to worry.

The next day was Christmas Eve. Clyde got off work at noon, and I took the day off so we could go that afternoon to see how Bob was. The day seemed hurried — we wanted to spend as much time as we could with Bob, but we also wanted to be back by 7:00 for the candlelight service at church.

Our visit was emotionally draining for all of us. Bob and Diantha were weighted down with tremendous bills so Diantha was working extra hours at her job in a nursing home. She had gone back to work the day after the surgery so today — Christmas Eve — Bob was all alone. Their son had just had his first birthday in December, and Bob had missed that. Now it seemed he was going to miss Christmas with his family, too. Because of the uncertainty, Diantha hadn't even put up a Christmas tree. No, there wasn't to be very much celebrating for my brother; the situation looked dreadfully bleak. Tears ran down my cheeks all the way home from the hospital because I felt so bad about leaving Bob on Christmas Eve. He was so lonely. Today at the hospital was the first time I had ever seen my big brother cry. My tears were also for myself. I thought that my stupid problem with bulimia was nothing compared to all the mountainous problems my brother had. Why couldn't I just be rid of these awful desires to binge and purge? Why?

I had pretty well pulled myself together by the time we got to the church for Candlelight Service. The ceremony was truly awe-inspiring. After Pat told the congregation a very touching story, and we sang some slow, tender hymns, we all stood in a circle holding our unlit candles.

Then Pat lit his candle and used it to light Debbie's candle next to him. One by one the candles around the circle were lit, and soon the room was filled with a soft, almost magical glow.

"The light you see in this room resembles the light of Jesus' love," Pat softly said when all the candles were lit. "It gets passed on to others through us . . . all of us. And that miraculous birth, so long ago, is the reason we are here today."

We closed the service, slowly singing 'Silent Night' in the soft glow of the candles. I looked around the circle and saw the faces of the people in the church, their eyes reflecting the light of the candles. Even the little children were silent during the closing prayer. I was sure I could feel the awesome presence of God.

My heart was filled with love at that moment for everyone there. I wished I could share the joy that I felt with my friends in Columbus, many of whom did not know Christ. There were so many people that God had used to touch my life that I wanted to thank, right then and there. My burden of bulimia was completely forgotten as I silently thanked my Savior, Jesus Christ. Oh, how I loved Him! He had been born to die for someone as unworthy as me.

Christmas day was hard to get through because of all the food, but it was also exciting. I got a very special Christmas card from Clyde. He wrote in it that he was thankful for all that God had done in our lives. He got me some very nice presents, too. The present that I loved most was a silhouette of Becky's head and shoulders made of construction paper. She had made it in pre-school, and she gave it to Clyde and me with such great pride, declaring her love and telling us that we were "the best mom and dad in the whole wide world!"

We spent the day visiting relatives. We went to Clyde's

mom and dad's for dinner with the usual holiday crowd, then to my parents home for supper and an exchange of gifts. At both places I tried hard to stay out of the kitchen and away from the food.

I had all these people in my family, and only my mom and dad knew about my bulimia. There was so much going on in their lives that I didn't want to tell them my troubles. Besides, I had Clyde, Bud, Pat, Debbie and my friends at the support group. They all loved me and wanted me to get over the bulimia. Soon I would be free, and no one would ever have to know.

By New Year's Eve Bob was home from the hospital. The church was having a party, but Clyde and I decided to bring in the new year with Bob and Diantha. We went to their house and had pizza and watched T.V. until 11:00, when Diantha got off work. Becky was tired and cranky, so we left soon after midnight.

Becky was asleep in the back seat on the way home. I looked at my husband, driving along in the darkness, and was keenly aware of my great love for him.

"I love you," I said quietly and reached for his hand.

"Good," he said, giving me a big smile and a firm squeeze on my hand.

I had so much that I wanted to tell him: how grateful I was for his putting up with my craziness all these months, that I was going to try my best to make it up to him for all the hardships I had brought on our marriage, that the worst was over and things could only get better because we both had come to love the Lord. I decided to just be quiet and enjoy the love that my precious husband had shown me.

January 1, Wednesday — This is a new year. New beginnings. Old habits thrown out. New directions. Learning to like myself and accepting my faults. My two New Year's Resolutions are:

1. To weigh myself only once a week.
2. To pray before I put *anything* in my mouth.

I think this is a turning point in my life. I'm always writing Pat and Debbie letters, hoping they will stop me from bingeing and vomiting. But they can't *do* it for me. The only person that can be responsible for changing me is ME. And it has to start with love, not anger, for myself in spite of my faults.

I feel like I'm on the way to recovery now for real.

PART III

HE MAKES

ALL THINGS

BEAUTIFUL

7

Metamorphosis

It was 1986 now — a new year, which I prayed would be better than any of the ones that had gone before. I began a daily Bible reading program in January, and my goal was to finish the whole book in a year. As I began to make early morning reading a way of life, the Bible became much more to me than just another book. In my mind I vividly pictured the stories of the Old Testament in living color: I could hear God tell Noah to build the ark; I could feel Moses' anxiety when God chose him to lead the Israelites out of Egypt; I could see the power of God's mighty hand as He parted the Red Sea. My bulimia was, for now, in the past.

I got so involved in my study of the Bible that I gave up writing in my diary. Instead, I began to write questions about what I was reading and call Pat on the phone for the answers. At first he was happy to answer my questions and was proud that I was doing so well, but within a very short time he got tired of it and presented me with one of his Bible dictionaries so I could look up the answers myself.

Well, that wasn't good enough for me. The Bible dictionary didn't answer the kinds of questions that I had. "Why did God do this?" "Why did He allow this to happen?" "Why didn't God do this instead of that?" Instead of finding answers I just got more and more frustrated, so many calls to Pat continued.

Finally Pat's patience with me wore thin. About the middle of January I called his home in the evening with another question.

"Molly, I'm glad you want to know about the Bible," Pat said. "In fact, I'm excited. But it took me years of studying to learn what I know . . . I still don't know everything. You're too impatient. You want to know everything in the next five minutes!"

Pat just didn't understand. I couldn't explain why, but he was right. I DID want to know everything about the Bible in the next five minutes. I didn't think I was being unreasonable. After all, wasn't answering Bible questions part of a minister's job? Couldn't he see that my calls were really sincere questions from a searching heart?

The fourth Tuesday of January rolled around before I knew it. I hadn't been able to contact my friend, Ann, so I had made arrangements with my Columbus friend, Susan, to meet me for supper before the support group. Our friendship had flourished into a bond that could never be broken in the short time since she had shared the most guarded secret of her past in an effort to show me Jesus' love. We went to the same restaurant where Susan had taken me in September.

As we ate our meal I excitedly told Susan about my friendship and the Hall family, how Clyde and I were making friends in the church, and that I was reading the Bible every chance I got.

". . . and I haven't binged or purged since before Christmas!" I finished triumphantly.

Susan beamed. "Praise God!" she said. "I love it when He answers my prayers for other people. I'm just tickled pink that you're doing so well."

"I know, so am I! I just wish that all the girls in the group were doing better," I told her with a sudden twinge of sadness. "I feel so bad when somebody only

Metamorphosis 103

comes once or twice and then never comes back. It's like they think there's no hope at all ... I wish I had enough guts to tell people about Jesus like you do."

As I said this, I wondered if she had told anyone else about her past. Somehow I felt sure that she had.

"Be patient, Molly. Maybe you're not ready. Moses went for forty years before he found out what the Lord had planned for his life," Susan said, grinning. "Be patient and keep studying. Pray that He'll use you, and He will. I'm just sure that He has some very important job for you."

"Well, I hope He tells me what it is pretty soon," I answered. "I'm afraid I'm not very patient. Oh, yeah, I've been wanting to ask you — what's going on with your dad? Do you ever see him?"

Susan nodded, "Once in a while. I've told him that I forgive him for the past and that I pray for him, but I don't know where he stands with God," she said. "He knows what the Bible says. It's up to him to do something about it. We can't make anyone accept Christ as Saviour ... all we can do is love them. Jesus shows His love through His people."

"I know!" I said. "He gave me Cynthia Rowland on the radio — then the support group — then Bud Harbin — then you — and now He's given me Pat and Debbie!" I paused a moment, my mind carefully re-playing the scenes that God had taken me through in the past few months. "Sometimes I'm just overwhelmed by His love. I don't deserve any of it."

"Listen to me," Susan said. "You've been adopted as a daughter in God's family through Christ. God can give you anything He wants and that's all there is to it." Susan finished by thumping her finger on the table. "Period."

Before we left the restaurant, Susan and I paused to pray together for the girls at the support group. There were a couple of girls whom we were particularly concerned about. They were going through some battles that both Susan and I could closely identify with.

As I drove home from Columbus that night, my heart swelled with affection for the women in the support group. I had been attending now for several months and felt right at home, but I keenly felt the desperation of the newcomers. While I was driving through the darkness I prayed for each one by name and thanked God once again for the people there who were volunteering their time to help us climb out of our eating disorders.

Near the end of January the usual frustration about filing the proper forms for income taxes began. When I had won that new car in March of 1985, I hadn't even thought about having to report the value of the car to the IRS for income tax purposes. If it hadn't been for my mother's reminding me, I wouldn't have thought about it at all.

Clyde didn't say much about it, but I thought that we could probably get away with conveniently "forgetting" to write it down. To be sure, I called the sorority that had sold the raffle tickets and asked them if they had filed any kind of report with the IRS. The answer was "No". After that I called the dealer where I had gone to pick up the new car and asked them the same question. They gave me the same answer.

Happily I told Clyde not to worry: the IRS would never know if we didn't tell them. He agreed with me, and the matter was settled ... or so I thought.

We had planned to have my brother, Bob, figure out our taxes on February third. Before that day came, however, my mother called me on the phone and pelted me with some pretty alarming statements.

"What are you going to do if someone reports you? A lot of people know that you won that car. Remember — it was even in the newspaper! You could end up paying some pretty big fines if you don't report it."

After I thanked my mother with a note of indignation, I hung up the phone receiver with a bang.

"God, I wish she would mind her own business!" I said to myself. I was upset by what I perceived to be a mother's meddling, but in the back of my mind I knew she was probably right.

I went to the Halls' home the next afternoon. Debbie was out shopping, so I sat in the living room and poured out the circumstances of my present dilemma to Pat.

"If we have to report it we'll probably end up having to pay a thousand bucks! But if we don't we might get caught and end up paying even more than that in fines!" I said, slouching down a little further in the easy chair. "Boy, I almost wish I hadn't even won that stupid car!"

Pat looked me straight in the eye with a very somber expression, and in the next moment he made a statement that I will never forget.

"You need to pay it, Molly. Not because you're afraid you'll get caught... but because you're a Christian. You need to do what's right in God's eyes."

As soon as the words were out of his mouth I knew that he was right. When was I ever going to learn to seek God's will instead of my own?

On Saturday, February 3, I took the day off work and went to Bob's house, my purse bulging with income tax forms, W-2's and receipts. After a couple hours of calculating, Bob came up with the startling verdict —Clyde and I were going to have to shell out almost $1,000 in federal, state and city taxes!

I didn't have any idea how we were going to be able to accumulate that kind of money by April 15. With both of us working, Clyde and I brought in a pretty comfortable income but neither of us were very efficient money managers.

We always paid the bills first and then conveniently spent the remainder, most often forgetting to add to our savings account.

Clyde was at his mother's house when I found out the news so I took Becky home and put her down for her nap, my mind racing with questions the whole time.

Instead of sitting down and trying to figure out a solution to the income tax problem, I allowed the hateful bad Molly to take control once again. In a two-hour span of time I made the vicious circle from the kitchen to the bathroom three times and, in the process, consumed practically everything in the house that was edible.

It wasn't just the tax problem that was bothering me; there was something else, something that had been gnawing at my brain since my conversation with Pat Hall about the taxes. His words, "You need to do what's right in God's eyes" kept running back and forth through my thoughts.

You see, I had some other unpaid debts which, until that conversation, I would just as soon have forgotten. After hearing Pat's words I had gone back in my dusty trunk of memories to when I had first become bulimic. I vividly remembered another terrible habit which I had acquired at the same time — stealing.

Before Clyde came home and while Becky was still asleep, I called Pat. I tried to talk in a normal voice, but it was difficult because I was upset about the taxes, the stealing and now the added guilt of bingeing and vomiting all afternoon.

"What if someone had been a thief and had stolen lots and lots of times before he became a Christian?" I asked, trying to conceal the fact that I was talking about myself. "Would God want him to pay back the people they had stolen from?"

"Well," Pat began slowly, "let's think about this a

minute... When you accept Jesus as your Savior then ALL your sins are forgiven, right?"

"Yeah, I know that," I said. "But what if he keeps on thinking about it and can't get it out of his mind — what then?"

"I guess he would have to pray about it and do whatever he felt that God wanted him to do."

"But what if there was a whole bunch of people he had stolen from," I continued, "so many that he couldn't remember them all? And even if he could remember, what if he died before he got them all paid back?"

After what seemed like an eternity of silence, Pat answered. "God knows everyone's heart. God would know he was trying. Remember, it's not the things we do that save us, it's God's grace."

I thanked him again and hung up. Nobody knew about my stealing but me and the owner of the store where I had been arrested two years before. Even though I hadn't told Pat, I was sure he knew whom we were talking about — and that her name was Molly Saunders.

I sat down with a piece of paper and began writing one by one the names of the people and stores with the approximate amount of what I had taken beside each one. There were so many! The total of my stealing debts was several hundred dollars. Certainly God wouldn't want me to pay them all back. Clyde and I were going to have a hard enough time just paying the income tax!

Clyde came home from his mother's, and I told him about the taxes. We sat down and calculated the amount of money we would be earning in the next few weeks before the taxes were due. It was clear to see that we would only be able to squeeze out enough money if we made some drastic cutbacks: no more diet soft drinks and no more eating meals out. It looked like baloney sandwiches or soup would be our meals for a while.

On top of all that, Clyde went to the kitchen for something to eat and, of course, the refrigerator was empty. He shoved the door shut and just glared at me. He knew what I had done without my having to say a word.

"GOD, IF HE KNEW ABOUT MY STEALING HE WOULD REALLY HATE ME!"

The situation was pretty bleak. We went to bed that night without talking. Clyde didn't have to say a word. Nothing could make me feel worse than I already did.

On Monday I went to Pat's office and confessed that it was really me that we were talking about on the phone. When he said that he already knew, my shame moved me to tears.

"Why is being a Christian so hard?" I asked him. "Poor Clyde doesn't know that he's married to a criminal."

"You're not a criminal," Pat said. "Well, not exactly. You've never been convicted, have you?"

"No, but I sure deserve to be. And what about Clyde? I feel like I'm telling you something that I can't even tell my husband. Isn't that wrong?" I asked. "And how can I even think of paying back old stealing debts when we're barely going to have enough for our income tax?"

"Boy, Molly, you have more problems than I can handle," Pat said. "I'm not sure what to tell you. I guess that your stealing is between God and you . . . and the people you stole from. I don't think you'd better tell Clyde. I'm not sure how he would deal with it."

"Well, that's one thing I agree with you about. I can't even think about paying any of this back," I said, waving my list in the air, "until we get the income tax out of the way. I guess I won't be able to afford any cream-filled donuts for a while . . . of course I could always steal some," I finished sarcastically.

Later that week I told Debbie all about my troubles. As I told her, she held my head on her shoulder, and we cried together. It was almost as if she could feel the pain I was going through. After we talked it all out I felt much better. I was greatly comforted by the fact that Pat and Debbie Hall, my dearest friends, would be praying for me. I was also confident that they would never tell anyone.

Debbie's younger brother, who lived out of the state, was planning to be married on February 14, Valentine's Day. The Hall family would be gone for a week, and they asked me if I would feed their guinea pig and bring in the mail while they were gone. I was happy to oblige. This turned out to be convenient for me because it gave me an opportunity to go to their house early in the morning and just be alone with my Bible and my thoughts.

Pat and Debbie left on Monday, and the week went fairly smoothly, considering all the turmoil that was going on in my brain. My Bible became my lifeline for survival. I felt like this awful desire to binge had never been stronger, but I knew I had to stop myself. With the money situation at our house I had to be very careful.

Friday came quickly. It was Valentine's Day, a day that was supposed to be filled with sunshine and love. Pat and Debbie would be home the next day, and I could hardly wait to see them.

After work I went to the college for my appointment with Bud Harbin. I told him all about the taxes and the stealing debts. I made the situation seem extremely bleak and by the time the hour was almost over, I had probably used half of his box of tissues.

Bud opened his filing cabinet, pulled out a poster with a Bible verse printed on it, and handed it to me.

TRUST IN THE LORD WITH ALL YOUR HEART AND LEAN NOT ON YOUR OWN UNDERSTANDING;

IN ALL YOUR WAYS ACKNOWLEDGE HIM, AND HE WILL MAKE YOUR PATHS STRAIGHT.

PROVERBS 3:5, 6

"Just do what you feel God is calling you to do, Molly. God can use our sins and turn them around for His glory," Bud said. "See what that verse says: 'In ALL your ways acknowledge Him, and HE will make your paths straight.' Maybe God has a reason for wanting you to go back and make right what you've done wrong."

"That's easy for him to say," I thought. I shrugged my shoulders. Maybe Bud was right, but I didn't want to discuss it any further.

I asked Bud if he had seen my friend, Ann. I hadn't seen or heard from her for several weeks. Although I had been calling and leaving her messages, she had never returned my calls.

Then the bombshell hit. Ann had been doing so poorly that she had decided to check herself into the Eating Disorder Unit at a hospital in Cincinnati.

I left Bud's office and headed for Pat and Debbie's house to put the mail in. On the way I cried out in frustration to God.

"WHY, GOD? WHY DIDN'T SHE CALL ME? WHY DIDN'T SHE LET ME HELP HER? ANN IS SUCH A GOOD CHRISTIAN — IT'S NOT FAIR!"

I got to the Halls' home and after putting the mail in, I sat down at the table to write them a letter. The message I wrote didn't make much sense — it was just scrawling out angry and irrational thoughts. Pat and Debbie were gone; now Ann was, too. I felt all alone.

I got up from the table and went to the cupboard where the Halls kept their food. I would never binge on food that belonged to such good friends under normal circumstances, but this time I just gave up the fight. I didn't care any more.

What an awful Valentine's Day that turned out to be! My heart ached for Ann . . . also for myself. If it could happen to Ann it could happen to me, right?

Pat and Debbie came home the next day, and after crying it out to them I felt much better. I was able to be thankful to God that Ann was where she needed to be —where she could get help.

Pat did me a big favor that week — he gave me a key to the church. The rest of February and all during March I went there each morning before work. I would sit on the floor in back of the pulpit and read my Bible in the dim light above the baptistry. In all the present confusion of my life this was the one time when I felt at peace.

Clyde and I were able to save enough to pay the taxes, and on March 28 we sent the money in. I was glad to have it paid. Now I could concentrate on paying my stealing debts. I had carried the list around with me in a small, zippered pouch that also contained the contract that Pat had given me.

I got the list out and looked at it from time to time, dreading what I felt God calling me to do.

The first debt that I decided to pay back was a department store near my home. Before I went into the store I sat in my car and prayed:

"OKAY, GOD, I'M GOING TO DO IT. PLEASE GO WITH ME."

I went to the store manager and described how I had stolen a pair of jeans, probably five years ago. I explained about the bulimia and told him that I had become a Christian, that I had a long list of stealing debts, and that I felt that this was what God wanted me to do.

God, in His wisdom, had led me to a Christian man. As I sat there, fighting back tears, the man said that he didn't want the money.

"Your soul is much more important than a pair of

jeans," He said in a kind, caring voice. "Take the money and pay someone else on your list, or put it in the offering at your church." I thanked him, and he shook my hand, telling me that I was welcome in the store anytime.

It didn't take me long to decide what to do with the $20.00 that I had in my hands as I left the store. There was a young man in our church that was trying to raise money to go to Venezuela to be a missionary. I thanked God for the opportunity to use the money to help him in his desire to serve the Lord.

Each time I went to pay back one of the stores on my list, it got a little bit easier. My bingeing and vomiting was coming under control. I was feeling better about myself and was able to share the victories over bulimia with my friends at the support group. I had gained some weight and wasn't particularly happy about that, but Susan wisely told me that God loved me no matter what size my clothes were. Sometime in March I gave my scales away. It was like giving away another burden. No more letting a number on the scales determine my mood for the day. I was beginning to experience a brand new feeling — freedom!

Everyday on the mail route I drove right by the store where I had been arrested. The store was on my list to be paid back. Even though I had lied to the store owner at the time, it really wasn't the first time I had stolen from him.

One day in mid-April, I was listening to a Bible radio broadcast. Right when I was sitting at the traffic light in front of the store, the man on the radio quoted Ecclesiastes 5: 4-5 *"When you make a vow to God, do not delay in fulfilling it. He has no pleasure in fools; fulfill your vow. It is better not to vow than to make a vow and not fulfill it."*

I felt then that I musn't put it off any longer. That afternoon I called the store owner from the Post Office.

Metamorphosis 113

"Mr. Marsh, this is Molly Saunders," I said. "Do you remember me?"

"Oh, yes," he said. (I guess store owners never forget shoplifters, especially when they threaten to kill themselves.) He agreed to see me, so I went there straight from the Post Office. It was so hard for me to face him; he was the only one who knew that I was a thief.

"I'm sure you remember when I stole from you," I nervously began.

Mr. Marsh nodded.

"Well, I'm glad now that I got caught...I...I told you some lies. See, it wasn't the first time I had ever stolen anything, but it WAS the last. I was so scared that I never stole again." I paused, swallowed hard, then continued, "I had another problem at the time. I don't know if you've ever heard of an eating disorder called bulimia..."

When I said "bulimia," Mr. Marsh's eyes opened wider, and he said, "My niece has bulimia!"

I could feel my hair stand on end as he told me how his niece and her family were having such a hard time because of her problem.

My mind was racing, and my heart, pounding faster. GOD KNEW! That's why He wanted me to pay Mr. Marsh back!

We talked for a while longer. I told Mr. Marsh the reason that I had come back and confessed to him: that I had become a Christian and that I had him on a list of people I felt God wanted me to repay.

I told Mr. Marsh that I wanted to help his niece. He shook his head and told me that she lived in Columbus.

"That's even better!" I said excitedly. "That's where the support group that I go to is!"

I offered to get him the support group's newsletters, which I kept in my car, so he could send them to her. Mr.

114 *Bulimia! Help Me, Lord!*

Marsh thanked me, and I left his store. I was so excited that I wanted to jump and shout!

Immediately I went to the library and began writing this girl a letter. I didn't know anything about her except that her name was Nancy, that she was bulimic and that she was Mr. Marsh's niece. The letter was a long one; my thoughts poured out faster than I could write them down. I told her about my own struggle with bulimia and about how coming to know Jesus Christ had changed my life. I explained how I had gotten arrested in her uncle's store and that the way I had found out about her was surely part of God's plan. I just knew that God wanted me to help her. I told Nancy all about the support group: how long I had been going, where the meetings were held and how often they met. As I wrote my address and phone number on the page, I prayed, "Lord Jesus, thank You. Please, please let me help Nancy!"

I took the letter to Mr. Marsh the next afternoon. I prayed that he would send it to Nancy. I would have sent it myself, except I didn't know her last name or her address. I wasn't even sure he would send it to her. Maybe he wouldn't want his niece hanging around with a former shoplifter.

After leaving the store, I drove straight to Pat and Debbie's house.

"You guys aren't going to believe this!" I yelled, bursting through the door.

Pat and Debbie's faces shone in amazement as I told them about the events of the past two days in a stream of run-together sentences.

"I have to tell Clyde now!" I told my friends. "I don't know how he's going to handle it, but this is too big to keep secret from him anymore. Pray for me, will you?"

That night I told Clyde. Admitting that I had been a thief was almost as difficult as telling him about the bulimia. I told him about the arrest and tried to explain why I hadn't told him about it until now.

Clyde got angry at me — and at Bud, saying that Bud didn't have any business telling me to pay them back.

"You can't dig up your whole life's mistakes!" he said angrily.

"Bud didn't tell me to do it. Nobody did!" I came back at him, defending Bud. "God had a reason for having me pay them back."

When I finished the story with the events at Mr. Marsh's store, I could see that Clyde didn't share my enthusiasm. He seemed to be hurt because I had done the stealing in the first place and also by the fact that I had told other people about it without telling him. I decided not to pursue the subject any further. I wondered if I should have kept it a secret after all.

Thursday, May 1, 1986 — Thank you, Lord, for this gift of food. Please help me eat moderately and wisely. Help me through this meal and the rest of the day. Amen.

This is a prayer that I composed back in September. The battle with bulimia goes on, but I feel victory so near that I can almost reach out and touch it. In January I stopped writing my diary because I thought I wouldn't need to. But now I WANT to, so I won't forget all the battles and especially *all the victories!*

I wrote eleven pages in my brand new diary (my third), compactly describing all that had happened since I had retired my last diary to the bottom of my dresser drawer, along with my first one. I got the old ones out and leafed through the pages, able now to see and rejoice in the changes that God had brought into my life.

Clyde seemed to forget what I had told him about the

stealing, and I felt as though it was something between me and God. Even though I knew he couldn't see the miracle of God's hand in my finding out about Nancy, nothing was going to take away my joy over the situation. I was sure that the Lord had taken my sin of stealing and turned it around for His glory, just like Bud had said!

On Sunday, May 4, I went to the evening church service, and Debbie met me at the door. After giving me a big hug, she took hold of my hand and said, "Come with me, lady!"

Debbie practically dragged me into Pat's office, saying that she had something to give me. She opened her purse and pulled out an envelope with an odd-shaped lump in it. She held it out to me with a huge smile on her face.

Another present! How exciting! Inside the envelope was a card . . . and a pin shaped like a butterfly. Its delicate golden wings were laminated with an iridescent blue coloring, and as I turned it in the light of Pat's office, it sparkled with all the colors of the rainbow. Its beauty was breathtaking.

My eyes could barely focus on the words in the card. Why? Because of my tears, of course.

Dear Sis,

Real beauty is not on the outside, but on the inside. Remember how you used to feel about yourself? Ugly, fat, worthless? You thought you were a horrible worm, right? But I praise God because I see you changing. You're allowing God to work in your life, and He's making you beautiful, just like a caterpillar when it changes into a butterfly. I love you, Sis, and I thank God that He's given you to me for my friend.

Love, Debbie

P.S. Keep on seeking Him. Let Him change you. He's doing a great job!

8

Surely Not Me, Lord!

During the next few days I was filled with excited anticipation. If I had been an eye-witness to the parting of the Red Sea, I couldn't have been more certain of the power of God. I wrote Ann a long letter and sent it off to the hospital in Cincinnati, then called Susan and several of my other close friends from the support group. The astounding story of how I learned about Nancy was too big for me to keep secret.

"I don't know if you believe in God, but..." was how I began. A couple of my friends didn't know what to say, and I sensed that they thought I was making the whole thing up. I didn't care. "... just you wait until the next support group! Nancy will be there, and you'll see that I'm telling the truth!"

When I went to see Bud Harbin at the college on Friday, May 9, I ran all the way from the parking lot and burst into his office, totally out of breath. I smiled at his startled secretary and tried to sit quietly until Bud was ready to see me.

"Bud, you'll never guess in a million years!" I began as soon as I closed the door behind me. Bud's face lit up, and his expression developed into a wide smile as I told him my story. With great animated gestures I related to him the radio broadcast and going to Mr. Marsh's store. I excitedly concluded with finding out about Mr. Marsh's niece.

"Gosh, Molly! God is doing lots of amazing things in

your life, isn't He?" Bud said, still smiling. "You ought to write a book."

"Yeah, I ought to!" I answered. Then I stopped. "But I couldn't. I mean . . . well, you know. Nobody knows about me. I couldn't write a book — then EVERYONE would know. And even if I did write my story, I COULDN'T tell about the stealing. If they found out at the Post Office, I'd lose my job."

Bud nodded. "Yes, I guess you're right . . . but it's such a shame that you have to keep all these things such a secret."

"Yeah, it IS a shame," I said, grinning. "Oh, well. I can share it with you, Clyde, Pat and Debbie . . . and maybe now some of my support group friends will believe God's power when they see Nancy walk in the door!"

I giggled and, inside, was filled with glee as I pictured how surprised my friends' faces would look when Nancy showed up.

After my appointment with Bud, I tossed his idea back and forth in my mind. Write a book? Me? Not very many people knew I was bulimic — even fewer knew I had been a thief. My whole family would probably disown me if they knew the whole story. Besides, in less than three weeks — May 23 — I would be twenty-nine years old. I was sure that I was too old to start any project as big as writing a book. No, I guess my story would be known only to a choice few.

On Tuesday, May 13, I could barely keep my mind on my work at the Post Office. Debbie Hall had gone to a few support group meetings with me, and she was definitely going tonight. She wanted to meet Nancy as much as I did.

On the drive to Columbus, Debbie and I discussed the possibility of starting a support group in Mt. Vernon. Current magazine articles telling how many people were afflicted with eating disorders made me certain that I wasn't alone. Surely there was a need for a support group here.

"We could probably do it," I told Debbie, "but we'd have to find a building first."

"Why couldn't we have it at the church?" Debbie suggested.

"Then everyone would know that I have bulimia," I answered. "We'd have to have it somewhere else. Maybe the library."

"HAD bulimia, you mean! Look how far you've come, Molly. Couldn't you tell the people at church now?"

"Sure, I'll call them all together and say 'Hey, you guys, guess what I used to do? I used to spend half my life with my face in the toilet' " I laughed. "I can just see it now." I pictured the looks of horror that would be on the faces of the congregation if I were to tell them the gory details.

"Hey, listen, what did Pat and I do when you told us? We didn't think you were disgusting. Well, not too often," Debbie said with a chuckle. "The people in our congregation love each other because they love the Lord, right? Don't sell them short, Molly. Give 'em a chance!"

As we neared the support group, Debbie cautioned me not to be too disappointed if Nancy didn't come.

"You don't know anything about her, you know. Maybe she's not ready to deal with her problem."

"Yeah, I know. But God wouldn't have had me find out about her if He didn't want me to help her."

We got to the support group and Debbie went into the room where the family and friends' group was.

I went into the room for the bulimics and greeted several of my old friends with hugs as I looked around the room for new faces. There were two that I had never seen before, both sitting in their chairs and nervously staring at the floor. I said a silent prayer for them and wondered which one was Nancy. When the facilitators arrived, we went around the circle and introduced ourselves. I tried not to show my disappointment when I learned that neither of the girls was Nancy.

A couple of my friends were concerned about me because I had been so sure that Nancy would come.

"Don't worry about me," I told them. "She probably had something to do. I bet she'll be here next time." Actually I WAS a little disappointed. On the way home Debbie and I prayed that God would be with Nancy and give her the courage to come next time.

I had decided to take the day after the support group off work and stay home and sew myself some new clothes. My old style of dress was the same, day in and day out: blue jeans and t-shirts. Now I was experimenting with bright, sunny dresses and loud print shirts, and this year I was even going to wear shorts! I decided that God had given me two strong legs and if they weren't as shapely as a model's, so what?

I got started early that morning. I was making myself a jumpsuit. As I was sewing I listened to an old recording that had been my favorite as a child. It was a recording of the Bible story about Moses. When I was younger, I had always liked the part about the plagues and especially, the parting of the Red Sea. But today it was more than just a children's story.

The Lord had heard the cries of the Israelites. I was sure that He also heard the cries of all the people suffering from eating disorders.

"Who am I, Lord, that you should send me?" Moses asked God as he stood by the burning bush.

The man on the record certainly did a good job portraying the voice of God. A deep, sovereign-sounding voice replied, "I WILL GO WITH YOU. I WILL HELP YOU SPEAK AND TEACH YOU WHAT TO SAY."

I sat at my sewing machine and realized that I had a big decision to make that would not only affect me, but also my whole family. God had kept me alive through all the physical abuse I had done to my body. He had blessed me beyond measure, had proved His love for me time and time again. If He did it for me, He would do it for others.

"LORD, I DON'T KNOW WHAT YOU WANT ME TO DO ... I DON'T WANT MY FAMILY TO BE HURT ... WHAT IF THEY? ... I'M SCARED, JESUS ..."

The record on the turntable was going 'round and 'round. The story on it was over, and in that silent moment I felt the Lord gently tell me, "I WILL GO WITH YOU." Right then I knew; my decision was made. I got up from the sewing machine and looked at the clock. It was only 7:00 a.m.

I decided to make a call to Norma Fladen, the executive director of the Mental Health Association in Knox County. I had talked to her a couple of times before, seeking information about eating disorders. When she answered the phone, I asked her to meet me at a nearby restaurant for breakfast. To my surprise she said yes.

Norma was a kind, compassionate woman in her mid-40's. I found her very easy to talk to. She told me that the Mental Health Association had tried to start something for eating disorders a few years before and that there was very little interest.

"Yeah, but I could help! I think we could have it at my church. The building is great!" I continued to attempt to convince Norma to give it another try. "We could put an ad in the paper, and you could get us some pamphlets to hand out ..."

Norma smiled, "Slow down, Molly. If we're going to do

this we have to do it right. First of all, we would need facilitators."

"Well, I could be one, and Pat and Debbie could..."

Norma shook her head, "Let me see what I can do." She took a sip of her coffee and paused a moment. "How would you feel about letting the newspaper write a story about you? A personal account is likely to draw more attention, and it wouldn't cost anything."

I didn't know what to say. I'd have to ask Clyde what he thought. Did I want my name and my story about the bulimia in the paper? If I did, I'd have to tell my family first. I made Norma promise to wait until I called her sometime during the next week.

From that Wednesday morning breakfast through the evening of Saturday, May 17, I did a lot of talking with Clyde about the newspaper story and the support group. It was comforting to know that Clyde was behind me, whatever I decided to do.

The next step was to tell my brother and sister-in-law, Bob and Diantha. I went to their house armed with a prayer and some pamplets which explained all about bulimia. It wasn't as hard as I thought it would be, after all.

"I'm sorry that I didn't tell you before now," I said to Diantha. "It's harder to admit my faults to the people who love me."

Since Diantha was Clyde's sister, I left her with the job of telling Clyde's parents, which she graciously agreed to do. Diantha and Bob vowed their love for me, and each embraced me with a big hug. I smiled and breathed a sigh of relief on the way home. I was beginning to feel free of the burden of keeping my problems such a deep, dark secret. It felt great!

Well, the next step would be a mountainous one: the entire church would have to know about me if the building was going to be used for this project. First I'd have to explain to the elders about my bulimia and the importance of having a support group. Pat kindly offered to explain the situation for me, but I declined his offer. As hard as it was, I knew that I had to do this myself. I did ask Pat to come with me, though, for moral support.

I contacted the three elders of our church and asked them to meet with Pat and me before evening service on Sunday, May 18. Throughout the day I prayed that God would give me courage to say the things I needed to say. All three of the elders are kind, caring men, and I knew Pat was going to come, but I was still scared. On the palm of my hand I wrote the words of 2 Timothy 1:7, *"For God hath not given us a Spirit of Fear, but a Spirit of Power, of Love, and of a Sound Mind."*

Pat didn't come to the church when he was supposed to, and I ended up having to tell the elders myself. I was so nervous that all the things I had planned to say vanished from my mind, and I was able to tell only them a few basic details.

To my amazement, in a few minutes they had agreed. Pat got to the church just as we were leaving the Sunday school room where we had met; he was out of breath and apologized for being late.

I gave a yank on his tie and said, "Don't worry, it's already taken care of."

When I called Norma Fladen on Wednesday, May 21, she already had several people who were interested in volunteering. She would set up the newspaper interview in a couple of weeks if I was still willing.

"Well, I've come this far; there's no way I'm going to back out now," I told her. I was amazed at the way God was working things out.

Friday, May 23 — Today is my birthday. I'm twenty-nine. It's been almost a year since I heard

124 *Bulimia! Help Me, Lord!*

Cynthia Rowland on the radio. I praise You, Jesus, for the showers of blessings You continue to pour out on me in spite of my failures. Keep me strong, Lord, for without You I am so weak.

Sunday evening, May 25, the breeze was blowing in through the open church windows. Everyone was in a pleasant mood, and, instead of the regular evening service, Pat asked the congregation to share any recent blessings they had received. A few people told of answered prayers, and after a short span of silence, I felt that now was the time to "come out of the closet." I told about my struggle with bulimia, and how God had given me Pat and Debbie to point the way back to Jesus. I got the contract that Pat had given me out of my purse and read it to them. Blinking back tears I told how God had taken me from death and given me life, and how I hoped to share His wondrous love through the support group.

After I was finished talking, lots of people came over and gave me hugs and told me how brave they thought I was. I used to think they would reject me if they knew, but they didn't. They loved me!

I drove to the support group in Columbus on May 28, alone. I had so many things to share: the support group plans for Mt. Vernon, the upcoming newspaper interview, the support I had received from my church. I also hoped that Mr. Marsh's niece, Nancy, would be there.

Nancy wasn't there, but I didn't let it bother me. As I told the group all that had happened since the last meeting, their eyes got a little wider.

"Wow, Molly! You're doing miracles!" one of my friends said.

"It's NOT me, though," I quickly answered, "I'm not doing it; it's God's power that's opening all the doors."

The next day I went back to Mr. Marsh's store to ask

him about Nancy. It had been over a month since I had written her the letter. She hadn't come to the support group or called me. I was worried about her.

When I asked him, Mr. Marsh shook his head. He was vague about the details but said that she had never received my letter. He said that she had moved and that no one knew exactly where she was.

I thanked him and left. "How can I help her, God, if I don't know where she is?" I thought. I was angry. "God, I told lots of people about this! I wanted them to see that You had a reason for wanting me to pay back those people I stole from! Now they'll think I'm stupid, and they won't believe in You. And now I don't know if Nancy is dead or alive. I want so badly to help her."

A message came through in the midst of that prayer: "TRUST ME," the Lord whispered.

"OKAY," I thought. I looked up to heaven and gave Nancy's problems to the Lord. He knew where she was, even if I didn't. I would just have to pray for Nancy. That's all I could do.

9

Going Public Is NO Picnic

On Monday, June 9, I walked into the office of the Mental Health Association, confident that the Lord was in charge and would guide me safely through the interview. I had written down the things that I knew were important in dealing with eating disorders. I wanted, above all, to let people know that my recovery and my desire to help others came solely from my Heavenly Father. I had even written down scriptures: Philippians 4:13 — *"I can do all things through Christ who strengthens me."* Proverbs 3:5-6 — *"Trust in the Lord with all your heart and lean not on your own understanding, in all your ways acknowledge Him and He will direct your paths."* I was ready!

A woman came in a few minutes after I did with pen and note pad in hand. She was sophisticated and professional, the kind of woman who used to intimidate me. She politely introduced herself: her name was Debby Massa, the "Life-style Editor" of the Mt. Vernon News. I stood up and smiled as Norma escorted us into another room where we wouldn't be interrupted.

The three of us sat down at a large table, and Ms. Massa wrote down my name, saying, "I'm sorry, I don't really know very much about bulimia. Where should we start?"

I leafed through the handful of literature I had brought with me, selected a newsletter from the National Anorexic Aid Society and handed it to her.

128 *Bulimia! Help Me, Lord!*

"Bulimia is an addiction to binge-eating and, in my case, self-induced vomiting to get rid of the food. Some bulimics use excessive amounts of laxatives or diuretics. We almost all have an obsessive desire to be thin."

I stated my problem matter-of-factly and went on to say that this behavior was primarily in my past. I explained that bingeing and vomiting were just symptoms of underlying problems that needed to be dealt with.

I wasn't prepared for her response. I could see a look of shock in Ms. Massa's expression. I tried to explain that bulimia wasn't something that I enjoyed, but that it was an addiction. I tried to explain that overcoming bulimia involved tremendous emotional struggles and that I had found hope through other people with the same problem at the support group in Columbus.

I felt my confidence evaporating as Ms. Massa asked questions that seemed miles from the real issue: "How much did you usually eat during an average binge?" "How many times a day did you make yourself vomit?" "Why did it take you eleven years to realize that what you were doing wasn't normal?" "If you ate that much every day, how could you afford it? Good grief, it must have cost you a fortune!"

As difficult as it was, I was trying very hard to answer all of Ms. Massa's questions honestly. How could I tell her that stealing money and food had been among my past resources to support my habit? I decided that she didn't need to know about the stealing. After all, I could tell by her actions and expressions that her opinion of me wasn't very high. I answered her question by telling her that my job at the Post Office paid very well, and that if I wanted to binge I could always find a way.

"This isn't going the way I planned, God," I silently prayed. "Why can't I make her understand?"

"I'm amazed that since you're a diabetic you even

Going Public Is NO Picnic   129

lived through eleven years of this!" Ms. Massa said after we had discussed the medical complications of bulimia.

I wanted to tell her that the Lord had kept me alive through all those years for a reason, but I kept silent.

"Okay, so after you knew that you were doing all this damage to your body, is that when you stopped bingeing and vomiting?"

"I learned about the damage to my body *after* I got help. Before that I didn't know very much about bulimia, even though I had been bulimic for eleven years. There are STEPS you have to go through in recovery — you can't just STOP!" I felt myself becoming extremely irritated by her ignorance of eating disorders and by her apparent distaste for the whole subject.

All the things I had so carefully prepared for were hardly covered in our talk. We had wanted the story of a recovering bulimic to print in the paper so that others would come forward and seek help, but I knew from the interview that the story would be a far cry from what I had pictured.

"I don't think we'll use your name in the article," Ms. Massa said. "It would probably be in your best interest to remain anonymous. If I have any more questions I can reach you at the Post Office, right?"

I nodded and watched her fold her note pad and walk out of the office. I looked at Norma Fladen and couldn't find the words to express how disappointed I was with the interview.

"Don't be too upset if the article doesn't turn out like you thought it would, Molly," Norma said, lightly touching my arm.

I thanked Norma for her moral support and gave her a hug. I walked slowly out of the office, got in my car and closed my eyes.

"God, I thought You wanted to use me to glorify Your

name!" I prayed indignantly. "All the work I'm trying to do for You, God — is it all in vain? How can I tell anyone all the miracles You've done in my life if they won't even listen? She isn't even going to use my name in the article — not that I care, God. It'll probably come out sounding like I'm crazy anyway. I asked You to use me... I WANT to show people Your love. Is this how it's going to be?"

I looked at my watch. It was only 3:30. The interview had started at 2:30.

"Only one hour, God! One lousy hour to say all the things I had to say!" I thought, "She thinks I'm crazy; I know she does!"

I left the parking lot and drove to Pat and Debbie's house, got out and abruptly stalked into their living room. They were sitting on the sofa with a half-eaten pizza between them.

"Hi, Sis! How did the interview go?" Debbie asked. I sank down in a chair and poured out my frustration over the way the news interview had gone. I was still angry over the events of the afternoon and told Pat and Debbie that I knew I was right on the edge of another binge.

Debbie got up and gave me a hug. She and Pat shared my feelings as I told them how badly I thought the interview had gone.

"I know it's the devil telling you to binge. Don't do it," Pat said. "You've come too far to throw it all away now."

"What's the use?" I said. "I don't care anymore." I went to the sofa and grabbed a piece of pizza. I plopped down on the floor and took the first bite. I looked first at Pat, then at Debbie, as if daring them to stop me, feeling rebellion in its worst form. I took another big bite, then another.

Pat leaned back and spread his arms out on the back of the sofa. I searched his face, half-wishing that he would come over and jerk the pizza away from me.

"If you're going to binge, Molly, I'm not going to stop you," Pat said. He was so darn calm!

Debbie looked at me with tears in her eyes. "Molly, don't do this to yourself. Pat and I love you. That stupid interview isn't worth bingeing over."

"I don't really want the pizza," I said. As I put the piece of pizza back in the box, I began to cry. "I'm just so confused. You guys told me that God wanted to use me. I don't know what He wants me to do."

"I don't know either, but we both know that if you binge it will just make things worse." Debbie said. She got up and held me in a loving embrace for a few minutes.

"I'll be okay," I said. "Thanks. How do you guys put up with me?" I said good-bye and left, thankful that Pat and Debbie had been there to help me overcome the urge to binge again.

That night, when Becky had been read a bedtime story, I sat on the edge of her bed and held her hand as she said her prayers.

"Thank you, God, for Shauna and Lindsey and Renee and Jeremy and . . ." the list went on to include practically everyone she knew. I was about to tell her that she had said enough when she stopped praying. She looked up at me, then quickly closed her eyes and said, "God, please help my Mom stay on her diet."

I gazed at my daughter in wonder. Becky had found me alone in my bedroom many times crying out to God for strength. Even though she didn't understand my problem, she showed me through her prayers the extraordinary love of my child.

Clyde helped me see things in a different light. "Maybe the interview didn't go the way you planned, but I bet it'll help someone. Look on the bright side — a year ago you would've died if anyone had found out."

Clyde was right. The interview hadn't really been all that bad. How could I expect people to react when they heard about someone who ate huge amounts of food and then threw it back up? I smiled as I thought of the changes that the Lord had brought about in my life. I had come a long way from the frightened, self-destructive woman I had been a year ago.

During the week I kept an eye on each day's newspaper, not wanting to miss seeing the article. I was still concerned about how the article would turn out, and prayed that the Lord would bless Debby Massa and guide her in her writing.

On Friday morning I got a phone call at the Post Office from Debby Massa. I was pleasantly surprised by her friendly voice as she went over the information I had given her. As she read parts of the article to me over the phone, my apprehension was replaced by amazement at how good the article sounded! Could it be that the impression I thought she had of me was only a reflection of my own self-image?

I was smiling when I hung up the phone. The article would be in Monday's paper. What was I worried about? "Thanks, God, for helping me through this."

Over the week-end I told everyone who knew about the plans for a support group to be sure and buy a paper on Monday. "... and please pray that people with eating disorders will see it."

On Monday, June 16, I finished work and ran the two blocks from the Post Office to the newspaper shop in downtown Mt. Vernon. Catching my breath, I walked to the table where there was a stack of copies of the Mt. Vernon News.

I was surprised to see a bold headline right on the front page: "RECOVERING BULIMIC WANTS TO HELP OTHERS — PAGE 8."

I bought two copies, then turned around and dashed out of the store, down the street to the Mental Health Association and flung open the door of Norma Falden's office.

"Norma, it's in the paper!" Norma looked up from her typing and said, "Great! Let me see it!"

I handed her a copy of the paper, saw an empty space in the corner of the office and sat down on the floor. I quickly thumbed through the pages and was surprised to see that the article was almost half a page long!

"RECOVERING BULIMIC NOW HAS HOPES FOR BRIGHT FUTURE."

As I read the article a tear trickled slowly down my cheek. It was an honest story about my fight with bulimia, how I was recovering with the help of counseling, and that I was beginning to realize that I was a worthwhile person. It also said that the Mental Health Association was making plans to form a support group. God wasn't mentioned anywhere in the article, but I could see His love and power between the lines.

I closed my eyes and thanked my Lord for the article, praying that He would use it to help people who were suffering with eating disorders.

10

Victory!

One of the blessings that Clyde and I had received since becoming involved in the church was the friendship of Mike and Ellen Smith. One afternoon in June I went to their home to visit. They had become the proud parents of a little girl, Julie, born May 30. She was a beautiful baby, and I thought she was lucky to have Mike and Ellen for her mom and dad.

I stood with Mike and Ellen in the kitchen, reminiscing about how uncomfortable I used to be around them. I laughed as I told Ellen that I used to be jealous of how pretty she was, especially when she wore a certain wine-colored dress to church.

She left Mike and me standing in the kitchen and returned a few minutes later with that very dress in hand.

"You mean this one?" Ellen asked. "That's funny, I never thought I looked good in this color. Do you want it?"

"Get serious," I said. "You can't give me your dress!"

"C'mon, I want you to have it."

It didn't take very much prompting to get me to accept. I looked at the smiling faces of my friends and realized that only God could have made such a strong bond between us.

"I'd love it!" I said. "And I love you guys. Not just because of the dress but . . . well, you know."

136 Bulimia! Help Me, Lord!

On Saturday, June 28, 1986, my heart was dancing, praising the Lord for the changes He had made in my life. Tomorrow would be exactly one year since I had received Cynthia Rowland's book in the mail. The battle was won! I was free!

I drove to Pat and Debbie's house when I got off work, ran through their yard and bounded into the back door.

"Oh, victory in Jesus, my Saviour forever! He sought me and bought me . . ." I sang loudly and skipped into the kitchen.

Debbie was seated at the table busily writing something on a tablet. When she saw me she got up, threw her arm around my shoulder and joined me in singing.

Pat came into the kitchen and smiled. "What's going on, you two?"

"Tomorrow is the day! My day! It's been one year since I got that book in the mail!" I said. "Can I ask you a big favor?"

"Okay, shoot." Pat answered.

"Can I request 'Victory in Jesus' tomorrow for church? I know it's late, but . . ."

Pat put his hand on his chin and frowned. "I doubt it. Karl is the song leader tomorrow. He's probably got the songs picked out."

I tried not to show my disappointment. Then Debbie and I watched his face break into a mischievous grin.

"Had you fooled, didn't I?" Pat said smugly. "I think it's a great idea. Just tell Karl when you see him in the morning."

"You creep!" I said, playfully punching him on the arm.

"Yeah, creep!" Debbie said, hitting him on the other arm.

"I was only kidding!" Pat threw his hands up in surrender. "Don't kill me! I have to preach tomorrow."

"I'm sorry," I said seriously. "I really thank God for you ... and everyone else at church. They don't think I'm terrible at all!"

"Or ugly, or fat or disgusting or any of those other names you used to call yourself," Debbie said.

"Yeah, isn't it great? They love me!"

I gave them both a hug, turned to leave, and began to sing the song of Victory that had become 'my song': "Oh, victory in Jesus ..."

I woke early Sunday morning with a song in my heart. It looked like the day was going to be cloudy, but nothing could dampen my spirits. I rolled over and nudged my still-sleeping husband.

"Hi, Honey," I whispered, kissing him on the cheek. "I love you."

Clyde enveloped me in his strong arms and held me close, saying nothing. No words were necessary, for the bond between us had grown stronger than ever in the past year. He had stood by me, encouraged and loved me, and had been a tremendous help in my struggle toward wellness. In my opinion, he deserved a medal for all the support he had given me. Of all the gifts God had given me, I treasured my beloved husband most of all.

I had almost fallen back asleep when I heard Becky and my step-daughter, Sherri, talking to each other in barely audible whispers. Clyde heard them, too, and lifted himself up to look at the clock.

"Gosh, it's after 8:00. We'd better get up, or we'll be late for church," Clyde said. He gave me a quick kiss and got out of bed.

After a flurry of getting breakfast out of the way, getting dressed and locating our Bibles, we were able to arrive at the church a few minutes before Sunday School was to begin.

I walked proudly into the building with my family,

wearing the dress that Ellen Smith had given me. I asked Clyde to take Sherri and Becky to their classes while I looked for Karl. In addition to being the song leader, he was the teacher for one of the Sunday school classes.

I found Karl in his classroom, studying his notes and busily preparing for the morning's lesson. He looked up and smiled as I walked into the room. I explained the reason that today was a special day and that I wanted to officially request "Victory in Jesus."

Karl agreed to change the program just for me and we went to look for a hymnal to find the page number. As Karl looked down the alphabetical list of songs his face became a bit downcast.

"It's not in here, Molly."

"Let me see," I said, taking the hymnal out of his hands. As I looked down the page I realized he was right. "I can't believe it!"

"Maybe we could have someone sing it as a special next week," Karl offered. "I can sing. You want me to sing it?"

"No, that's okay," I said. "Jesus and all the angels are rejoicing with me today. I've been singing it in my head for a week anyway. Thanks."

I sat through Sunday school class, mentally praising the Lord. The chorus of "Victory in Jesus" kept floating through my brain. When class was over and the worship service was about to begin, I spotted Pat standing in the foyer. I told him that my song wasn't even in the hymnal.

"It's okay, though," I assured him. "Nothing could make me feel bad today."

The service began, and Clyde squeezed my hand as we sat together. I knew that, in his quiet way, Clyde was celebrating, too. I vividly recalled a conversation we had had together a few months before. I had asked Clyde, "If you could have a wish and get anything in the world, what would you wish for?"

After a few minutes of thought, he had replied, "I would wish for you to be completely free of your bulimia."

Today his wish was coming true. I had promised many times that I would never binge and purge again, but today I felt sure that I would be able to keep that promise.

After the opening hymns were sung the pianist began to play a selection of music as the offering plate was passed. My heart leaped as I recognized the music!

"She's playing 'Victory in Jesus!'," I whispered to Clyde. I joyfully sang to myself the words of the song that I loved so much.

When the service was over I asked the pianist if Pat had told her to play it.

She told me that she had just flipped through her music the night before and randomly picked it out. "Just a coincidence," she said, when I told her that I had requested that song.

"Coincidence, nothing!" I told her. "It's a miracle! God gave it to me! He really is celebrating today, I just know it."

I went around after church telling anyone who would listen what had just happened. My friends shared my enthusiasm as I let them in on my private miracle. I cherished every one of these people and thanked the Lord for my loving church family.

Clyde and I spent a lazy afternoon lounging in the sun, watching our daughters play in the wading pool in our front yard.

That evening there was to be a concert by a local gospel group at our church. Clyde had said that he was tired and didn't feel like going, so I asked him if he cared if I went alone.

He said that it was alright, and I went back to church

that evening, singing in my heart. I had had a wonderful day and felt glad to end the day listening to music.

The group was great. It was a uplifting performance by four women from a nearby church, whom I thought sang like the angels. I felt as if they were singing for me.

"We usually like to sing a hymn for our closing song," the leader of the group said when they were almost through. "And if you know it, we'd like to invite you to sing along. The one we've picked out we don't sing very often, but it's a beautiful song. It's called 'Victory in Jesus.' "

I think my heart skipped a beat or two. I was sitting near the back and half the congregation turned around and looked at me, excited smiles on their faces.

"God's done it again!" I thought. "Twice in one day!" I savored the miracle of God's love as I stood with His people and sang the words like I had never sung before.

The many people that God had sent to bless my life and help lift me out of my bulimia paraded through my mind, waving flags and carrying signs of victory. How I wished they could all be here to share this moment of happiness with me! God had given me my song, not just once, but twice. Hallelujah!

11

The Icing on the Cake

I was so confident that the Lord had given me 'Victory in Jesus' on June 29, that I was also sure He wanted me to write my story. He had given me a great ending!

Little did I know that the storm wasn't really over. I had been too involved in trying to hurry the Mental Health Association about the proposed support group in Mt. Vernon. So involved, in fact, that I failed to see the needs of my dear friend, Debbie Hall.

I was somewhat aware of the turmoil between Pat and Debbie, but I had no idea about the real cause of the problem. Unknown to Pat or any of the rest of her family, Debbie had become addicted to prescription drugs. In desperation she had gone to several doctors, feigning various illnesses to get her supply. The crisis came to a head during the second week of July when several events occurred which made it obvious to both of them that something had to be done. Pat had no choice but to contact a drug-rehabilitation hospital in Columbus. As hard as it was, Debbie admitted that she had a problem and reluctantly agreed to go.

The lives of the Hall family came crashing down around them and Pat felt that he had no option but to resign: how could a minister go on preaching when his wife had a problem with drugs?

The same love that the congregation had shown me when I told them about my bulimia flowed from the caring hearts of the people and engulfed Pat and Debbie in their time of need. We were able to convince Pat to stay, to let us help. The ladies of the church offered babysitting, cooking and housecleaning for Pat while Debbie was gone.

Although Debbie wasn't allowed visitors at the hospital, she received lots of flowers and was flooded with letters and get-well cards.

My own recovery from bulimia that I had been so sure of earlier came into question. All I could think about was the plain fact that my relationship with Debbie had been one-sided. She had done all the giving, and I had done all the taking. I felt sure that her problem with drugs was partly my fault. I cried out to the Lord in anguish for my friends. Why didn't Debbie tell anyone that she needed help? Why hadn't she come to me? I would have loved her no matter what she had done. In the midst of my pain for the two dearest friends I had, the symptoms of bulimia returned for a short time.

I soon realized, though, that the Lord had given me a whole network of people to help me see things more clearly. Bud Harbin, the people at church and my friends at the support group in Columbus helped me to be truly thankful that Debbie was where she needed to be — where she could get help. Coming to that awareness was good, but I was still bombarded with "bad Molly" thoughts. The pressures to binge and purge were almost unbearable.

I had begun to write my story before Debbie went to the hospital, but I had to give it up because I couldn't think clearly, let alone write. I told myself how stupid I was for ever thinking I could write a book: I had never gone to college; I couldn't type, and I wondered why I had even listened to Bud's foolish suggestion.

In an attempt to distinguish some kind of order in all

the confusion, I held fast to the one thing that gave me peace — the daily reading of God's Word that I had begun in January.

Early one morning during the first week of August, I sat at the table and opened my Bible. The pages fell open to the Psalms and my eyes focused on these words:

> *Come and listen, all you who fear God; let me tell you what He has done for me! I cried out to him with my mouth; his praise was on my tongue. If I had cherished sin in my heart, the Lord would not have listened; but God has surely listened and heard my voice in prayer. Praise be to God who has not rejected my prayer or withheld his love from me!*
> Psalm 66:16-20

My eyes were moist as I read the words. The events of the past year flashed in an instant through the back of my mind. The Lord had brought me from death and given me life, had done miracles about which only I could testify, and had poured out blessing after blessing upon me. He had given me a story to tell, and I had promised Him that I would tell it. I knew at that moment what I must do. With renewed conviction, I began again to write a few pages of my book each morning before work.

During the five weeks that Debbie was in treatment, I continually lifted the Hall family in prayer before the Lord and prayed that His love would hold the church together in this time of crisis.

On Sunday, August 24, Pat preached a sermon about love. One of the scriptures he used was Philippians 1:3: *"I thank my God every time I remember you."* Pat had great difficulty expressing his love and his gratitude for everything that the people of Central Church of Christ had done for Debbie and him. It was an extremely emotional sermon, and I was sure that there wasn't a dry eye in the church.

Then Pat gave us all the joyous news — Debbie would be getting out of the hospital the next day! The love of the Lord had bonded us together through the rocky storm, and now the clouds were clearing. Praise be to God!

I was filled with anticipation for Debbie's return, and the very next day, Monday, August 25th, I received another unexpected blessing. It was a letter from Cynthia Rowland, the author of *The Monster Within*. I had written to her several weeks before, asking permission to describe in my book the radio interview that had started me on the road to recovery. To my surprise she not only gave her consent but invited me to a weekend retreat for people who were recovering from bulimia. The retreat was to be held in Lindale, Texas, in October, and Cynthia was to be the featured speaker.

After figuring out the cost of the retreat, air fare and a rental car I saw little hope of being able to go, but I felt honored that I had been asked. As soon as I got home from work I called several of the church women and asked them to pray that somehow God would provide a way for me to go. Wouldn't it be wonderful if I could actually meet the first person God had used to guide me toward recovery?

Tuesday, August 26th, I could barely contain my excitement for two reasons. When I had told Clyde about the letter and the retreat the night before, he had told me to go ahead and send the reservation in! We both agreed that if the Lord wanted me to go, then with His help the expenses would somehow be taken care of.

The second — and best — reason that I was excited was that Debbie Hall was coming home! Tomorrow night the church would be having a surprise party for her. How my arms ached to give my dear friend a hug!

This was a special Tuesday — a truly glorious day. I drove to Columbus to the support group and couldn't

The Icing on the Cake 145

wait to tell my friends about the letter from Cynthia Rowland and the retreat. The retreat was for people recovering from bulimia so I took the information along in hopes that someone else would go.

The whole group listened attentively as I read the letter from Cynthia and then told them about the retreat.

". . . I don't even know for sure if I'm going, but if anyone's interested you could write the number down and call. Who knows? Maybe a group of us could go."

The group was very large that night — so many of us that several were sitting on the floor. A young blonde woman who was sitting on the floor right across from me timidly introduced herself as Nancy, saying that she'd like to have the number.

My heart skipped a beat when she said her name . . . and my mind raced back to my conversation with Mr. Marsh, the owner of the store where I had been arrested for shoplifting. Could this attractive, shy young woman be Mr. Marsh's niece?

"You don't have an uncle who owns a drug store in Mt. Vernon, do you?" I asked, holding my breath and waiting for her response.

Nancy looked at me, her eyes wide with the wonder of the knowledge that she and I shared.

"Are YOU the one that got caught . . . ," she stopped in mid-sentence, looking around the group as if embarrassed for me.

"Yes! Yes!" I said. "Oh, Nancy, I've been praying for you for months! Where have you been?"

More than half of the group had absolutely no idea what we were talking about. For at least thirty minutes we unfolded the story for the rest of the group, Nancy filling in the parts that I didn't know.

Nancy said that she had called her mother, Mr. Marsh's sister, and found out about me. Even though the

146 *Bulimia! Help Me, Lord!*

letter I had written to her had been lost, and Nancy didn't even know my name, she had been encouraged by hearing about my recovery. The whole group was caught up in the excitement of the story that Nancy and I shared. I wished that I could stand up and tell my friends what I was feeling in my heart. God knew! God had answered my prayer to enable me to help Nancy, but in His time, not mine.

After the group was over Nancy and I hugged and talked as if we were old friends. She was going to ask her parents for financial support so that she could go to the retreat in Texas.

I knew then that I just HAD to go! On the way home from Columbus I praised God for Nancy and prayed that things would work out so that we could go together. I even stopped at a convenience store to buy an instant lottery ticket. Well, who knows? Maybe God could answer my financial prayers with lottery ticket winnings. I mean, if I won a few thousand dollars I could take the whole support group with me to Texas.

"You won't believe this," said the clerk when I told her what I wanted, "but we just sold the last one. It's the very first time we've ever run out. Sorry."

I went back to my car feeling embarrassed before the Lord. "Okay, I get the message, God," I thought. "But please, please work this thing out."

The next day, Wednesday, August 28, was the party for Debbie. I was so excited — I wanted to tell Debbie and everyone else at church about my chance to go to Texas and about Nancy. Clyde had shared my enthusiasm when he had heard about Nancy but had made me promise to keep the news quiet until later. I knew he was right. This party was for Debbie, not me.

Someone had made a huge banner that said, "WE LOVE YOU PAT AND DEBBIE!" and had stretched it across the wall of the church basement for the party. Debbie walked in for what she thought was Bible study and was so overwhelmed with love and hugs from the congregation that she couldn't hold back her tears.

Debbie wasn't the only one crying. Many of us were deeply moved with gratitude because our prayers had been answered, and Pat and Debbie's family was back together at last!

I tried to keep the news about Nancy and the retreat to myself during the party, but I just couldn't. When I saw Ellen Smith take her daughter to the nursery, I followed her and told her the whole story.

"You have to pray real hard now, Ellen," I begged. "If Nancy can go, I just HAVE to go with her!"

During the next few weeks, I told practically everyone I knew about the retreat. My constant prayers were for Nancy and me to be able to go to the retreat together. The proposed support group in Mt. Vernon was also on top of my thoughts, and I prayed that the Lord would send enough volunteers to make it a success.

In an amazing three-week chain of events too lengthy to describe, my church, a sister church in Columbus and my family and friends raised exactly enough money for my whole trip!

I made friends with Nancy's parents and was excited to find out that they were going to help her financially so that she would be able to go with me. I also went to Mr. Marsh's store and told him with confidence that I just knew Nancy would soon be victorious over her bulimia.

Imagine! When I had been arrested in his store I was scared to death of this man. Now I had become great friends with him and affectionately called him "Uncle John."

It seemed as if I was being pulled in many different directions. The plans for the retreat had me so excited that I was barely able to sleep. This was going to be the first time I had ever been on an airplane, and I was going with Nancy to meet Cynthia Rowland!

The Mental Health Association had put me on a committee for planning the support group, so I had that on my mind, too. I tried to think of a name for the group. We had to have a name, didn't we? We needed a friendly sounding name that would be easy to remember. After trying out several, I came up with one that I thought was great: Friends Recovering from Eating Disorders . . . FRED.

For several days I mulled the name over in my mind. It had a nice ring to it. I wasn't sure that the people from the Mental Health Association would like it, but I planned to suggest it to them sometime in the future.

Early in the morning on October 24th, Nancy and I were on our way to Lindale, Texas. During the flight the sun shone gloriously. I kept wanting Nancy to pinch me to prove that I wasn't dreaming. I got to sit by the window on the plane, and I saw the magnificence of God's handiwork as my eyes beheld for the first time the tops of clouds!

The weekend was an experience I will never forget. Nancy and I grew to love each other like sisters, and I got to meet and hug Cynthia Rowland! There were many special, caring people at the retreat, each one in a different stage of recovery. There were so many, in fact, that I didn't get a chance to tell Cynthia Rowland about the degree to which God had used her own testimony to touch my life. Although we live on opposite sides of the country, I love her deeply. I hope that some day she will read my book and share the joy of all that has occurred in my life since I heard that radio interview on that hot, muggy day in June, 1985.

I heard a speaker on the radio a while back talking about the Israelites when they were in bondage to the Egyptians. He said they were God's children, that God loved them and heard their cries for mercy. He felt their pain, and when He could bear their misery no longer, He sent someone to deliver them from their bondage.

That story is true of me. The Lord has always loved me, and I'm quite sure that He felt the pain that I endured during all my years of turmoil. I just didn't know how to reach out to Him. And when He could bear my misery NO LONGER He sent not just one, but many precious people to deliver me from my bondage.

I have seen God's miracles. I have felt the deep love that binds together the hearts of those who believe in Jesus Christ and have accepted Him as Lord and Savior.

I pray the Lord will use my life and my story to bring people to Him, the greatest source of healing. I would like to close this story that the Lord Jesus has given me to tell you with this beautiful little scripture that has become my prayer for all those who struggle with life's complex problems:

May God grant you the desires of your heart and make all your plans succeed. We will shout for joy when you are victorious! We will raise our banners to God for all He has done for you.

Psalm 20:4-5

IF YOU HAVE AN EATING DISORDER . . .

If you've never admitted it to anyone before, I know you're frightened. I know that you sometimes feel like you are all alone and that nobody cares for you or loves you. Maybe you've prayed that God would heal you instantly, and that prayer hasn't been answered. Perhaps you thought that reading this book would show you some magical cure that would make you better. Believe me, I wish it could.

I pray that reading my book has inspired you. I hope that it has planted deep within your soul a seed of faith that God has the power to change lives if we let Him, no matter what the circumstances. But believe this: God works through people. There are places that deal with eating disorders in every major city across the United States. They say the first step is the hardest, but you have to make it if you want to be free of your eating disorder. *"The way of a fool is right in his own eyes, but a wise man is he who listens to counsel"* Prov. 12:15.

If you think that you will outgrow the behavior, don't be fooled. The problem isn't just with the starving or bingeing and purging; those are just symptoms. The real problem is the underlying issues, the hurts and angers that you've experienced that keep you trapped in your eating disorder.

Reach out to someone who is able to help you see things more clearly. I also want to encourage you to become involved in a support group where you can share both the struggles and victories of recovery with others who've been there.

Healing takes time, work and determination. The healing process involves a series of advances and setbacks. When a setback is experienced it can be used as a learning tool and although it seems like a long, difficult process, please don't give up: TOTAL RECOVERY IS POSSIBLE.

Even though I may not know you personally, I love you. More importantly, the God of all creation loves you with an everlasting love. Get into His Word and believe His promises. May the Lord comfort you, guide you, strengthen you and give you the courage to overcome.

Love, Molly

The Icing on the Cake

So do not fear, for I am with you;
Do not be dismayed, for I am your God.
I will strengthen and help you;
I will uphold you with my righteous right hand.

Isaiah 41:10

Just a Few Closing Words

Learning. Changing. Growing. Seeking to become what God wants me to be. Looking for ways to show people His marvelous love. These are the attitudes that I pray will be the focus of my life always.

On May 23, 1987, I celebrated my thirtieth birthday. (Funny, I don't feel "over the hill" at all!) During a time of prayer and reflection on my birthday I wrote this poem:

My Parade

Oh, the splendor and beauty I find
When I close my eyes to see
A wondrous work of His mighty hands;
A parade He has given to me.

Every Christian has one, too,
A parade of his very own,
Of friends who shared the story of Jesus
And helped him make heaven his home.

There are people of every description
Dancing through my mind;
Singing and shouting a victory tune
Because I am no longer blind.

The biggest desire of my life now
Is helping others to see
The Savior who changes our lives on earth
And gives us the victory!

My parade continues to grow, my friend,
   With each person I chance to meet.
Oh, won't you listen to His precious words
   And kneel at Jesus' feet?

The grandest parade of all will be
   When old things have passed away,
And my Jesus leads the parade in Heaven
   On that bright and glorious day!

Thank You, Jesus

If God uses my book to help you see and accept Christ I will be proud to dance and shout in *your* parade!

And just so you'll know, Friends Recovering from Eating Disorders (FRED) is now a Christian organization here in Mt. Vernon, of which I am proud to be a part. I am thankful for the dedicated volunteers who desire to serve the Lord by helping people who struggle with eating disorders.

We have a free bi-monthly newsletter, the **FRED MAILBAG**, of which I am currently the editor. If you would like to receive the **MAILBAG**, further information on various organizations designed especially for those who have an eating disorder, or just to contact me you can write to:

Friends Recovering from Eating Disorders
1005 Harcourt Rd.
Mt. Vernon, Ohio 43050

Anorexia Nervosa and Bulimia: a Comparative Review

By Amy Baker Enright, M.A. and Randy Sansone, M.D.

This article is designed to provide the reader a brief overview of anorexia nervosa and bulimia, the medical and psychological complications, and treatment alternatives.

Amy Baker Enright is Executive Director of the Bridge Foundation, a non-profit organization which manages the National Anorexic Aid Society and the Center for the Treatment of Eating Disorders, in Columbus, Ohio. Randy Sansone is Director of the Eating Disorders Unit, Sycamore Hospital, Dayton, Ohio.

This article is included in this book with the permission of the National Anorexic Aid Society.

ANOREXIA NERVOSA

Anorexia nervosa has been described as the "self-induced starvation syndrome." Laymen often refer to it as "dieting gone wild" or "dieting out of control."

The weight loss is achieved through a variety of methods, most commonly severe calorie restriction and fasting. Weight loss methods can include excessive diuretic and laxative use, self-induced vomiting, relentless exercising, and the use of various over-the-counter and prescription diet aids.

The obsession with dieting is maintained because of the distorted attitudes about the meaning of weight loss, thinness and eating. The anorexic feels she is in a turbulent and inconsistent world, full of demands and expectations. Amidst this confusion lies one anchor of sameness — her body. She uses her body to shift her attention from the perceived expectations of others to new expectations of herself.

However, the shift is a trap. By refocusing her energy on weight loss, she still has not confronted her fears and needs in interpersonal relationships. Therefore, she has replaced an outside world of standards and expectations with an inner world of standards and expectations. Neither can resolve her interpersonal dilemma.

Psychologically-induced weight loss (starvation) may cause a variety of physiological changes. In an attempt to maintain the functioning of the most critical organs (the heart and the brain), the body begins a conservation program and slows down or stops less vital physiological processes. These may include the absence of menstrual periods, lowered heart rate and body temperature, lowered blood pressure and respiratory rate, constipation and diminished thyroid functioning.

In addition, "lanugo," fine, baby-like hair, may appear on the skin, in the body's effort to conserve heat.

The body must also deal with the complications of weight-loss methods and malnutrition. Unfortunately, the body has limitations in its ability to withstand these regimens. Mortality rates due to anorexia nervosa have been documented as high as 10%.

Anorexia tends to develop in early adolescence and early adulthood. Ninety-five percent of the victims of anorexia nervosa are women. Characteristics of anorexia nervosa may include distortion of body image (the perception of being fat in the face of emaciation), hyperactivity (rigorous excessive exercising and increased activity level which is present in a starvation state), and hunger denial (the blocking out of feelings of hunger while being preoccupied with food).

BULIMIA

Bulimia, the sister disorder of anorexia nervosa, translated from Greek roots means "ox hunger," and is characterized by binge-eating. Binge behavior consists of the secretive, frenzied consumption of large amounts of high calorie or "forbidden" foods during a brief period of time (usually less than two hours).

Commonly, the binge behavior is counteracted by a variety of weight control methods (purging), including self-induced vomiting, diuretic and laxative abuse, and rigorous exercise. These binge-purge cycles are normally followed by self-deprecating thoughts, depressed mood, and an awareness that the eating pattern is abnormal.

Unlike the anorexic who uses these methods for weight loss, the bulimic employs these techniques for weight maintenance. Although bulimics may be up to 15% over or under normal weight, according to the Metropolitan Life Insurance tables, their focus is not excessive thinness. They acknowledge their hunger and do not exhibit the body image distortion of the anorexic.

For the bulimic, food often takes on symbolic meaning and may be an outlet for feelings of frustration, disappointment, anger, loneliness and boredom. They literally fill these voids with food, but then must struggle with the issue of weight gain. The binge-purge cycle is thus continued. Food becomes the bulimic's best friend and worst enemy. Unlike the anorexic, who turns away from food in an attempt to cope, the bulimic turns to food to cope. To the anorexic, eating is a controlled choice; for the bulimic, eating is an embarrassing and uncontrolled impulse.

The process of purging has its medical consequences. Vomiting, and the excessive use of laxatives and diuretics, not only cause dehydration and its accompanying symptom of lightheadedness, but can result in hypokalemia (low levels of potassium in the body). Hypokalemia may result in fatigue, seizures, heart arrhythmias, and hypokalemic nephropathy (kidney damage directly related to chronically low levels of potassium).

Vomiting may cause irritation to the esophagus, precipitate swelling of the salivary glands, and have dire consequences on the teeth. Unlike anorexics, bulimics do not usually lose their menses, but menstrual irregularity may appear at times and is most frequently due to excessive stress.

Bulimia tends to develop in late adolescence and early adulthood. Bulimics tend to be older than calorie restrictors, and they may previously have been anorexic. Ninety-five percent of the victims of bulimia are women.

The major differences between anorexia and bulimia are:

1. Anorexics deny their eating disorder; bulimics are aware of their abnormal eating patterns.
2. Anorexics deny their hunger; bulimics are acutely aware of their hunger.
3. Anorexics feel fat even though they are excessively thin; bulimics rarely exhibit a distortion of their body image.

Unlike the anorexic who is identifiable due to severe weight loss, the bulimic may remain hidden from others and alone in his/her struggle.

Many people have characteristics of both bulimia and anorexia nervosa. They may also alternate between times when they appear to have symptoms of anorexia and symptoms of bulimia.

The majority of persons who present themselves for

outpatient treatment are bulimic. Most anorexics request help when other people encourage it or insist that they come. Both disorders are treatable and require a multi-dimensional approach to treatment, of which intense psychotherapy is the foundation.

THE INTERPERSONAL DILEMMA IN EATING DISORDERS

There are uncanny similarities among those suffering from eating disorders. In early childhood, both anorexic and bulimic individuals perceive similar "family messages" or "rules of the road." Often the child interprets these messages in a distorted way.

While there is a family message to achieve and excel in the world, the child often "hears" that perfection is the minimum standard, and that rewards and special attention can only be received from the family by surpassing this standard. Therefore, the child initially seeks attention and acceptance by trying to be better than perfect.

This style of dealing with the family and the world makes her appear like "THE BEST LITTLE GIRL IN THE WORLD." This compliance fosters enmeshment (intense engagement) with the family. The family becomes her barometer for self-esteem. But, the child constantly finds herself falling short of "expectations." There is the ever-present double-bind: perfection is the minimum; perfection is impossible. This situation leads to feelings of inadequacy, incompetence, frustration and anger.

By the time of adolescence the external world begins to replace the family as the barometer for "success". It not only reinforces the early messages learned at home about appearance and performance, but, the "ante" for social success has greatly increased.

To society, being a successful woman engenders all

those impossible feats portrayed in the media — "super woman." This "super woman" is not only competent in her career and social/love life, but is the peak of visual perfection. Society places no premium on feelings or emotions but does emphasize figure, stylishness and social sophistication.

Most of the time, the adolescent is not developmentally prepared to live up to these rigid social expectations. "Force feeding" of these expectations prevents emotional growth and inhibits self-actualization — the process by which an individual achieves true self-acceptance and intimacy with others. The inability to engage in this process leaves feelings of "emptiness" and inadequacy.

Both the anorexic and bulimic focus on their bodies to cope with feelings of inadequacy. It becomes the one arena where they can obtain a personal sense of mastery.

ANOREXIA-NERVOSA

The anorexic becomes obsessed with thinness and turns away from food in an angry attempt to avoid dealing with society's aspirations for her to be "super woman." She rejects the feminine role and figure. Her thinness retards psychological maturity and she appears pre-pubescent. In her emaciated state, she becomes unappealing to men and thereby avoids the issues of intimacy, rejection, and sexuality. She can maintain a childlike appearance and remain dependent upon her family to meet her needs. The empty stomach, the void, provides a sense of control and power.

The anorexic is proud of her thinness and her ability to conquer hunger. This provides her with an inner source of self-esteem and control. Yet there is the anger: the anger with parents and society for setting standards and expectations that are seemingly unattainable.

The anger is often expressed through social isolation,

introversion, denial, and a pseudo-compliance coupled with hostility. The denial is pervasive, particularly in the area of body image, hunger, and acknowledging the illness. Denial allows the anorexic to continue on her fixed course and maintain a facade of control.

BULIMIA

Unlike an anorexic, who negates the "super woman" concept, the bulimic concentrates her energy on fulfilling the role of the "ideal woman". This results in an intense focus on the "outer shell," a preoccupation with appearance and performance. Feelings and emotions are submerged beneath the "shell" and are often difficult to get in touch with.

The world (Society) becomes the bulimic's barometer for approval. In an attempt to please everyone, she becomes paralyzed in decision-making because of multiple alternatives given to her by society. When the tension becomes overwhelming, she releases her frustration through impulsive behavior. The impulsivity may take the form of shoplifting, sexual indiscretions, drug and alcohol abuse, and episodes of binge eating. For many women, food not only fills the void for feelings of frustration and anger but also for loneliness and boredom. Bulimics turn to food to cope.

In relationships, bulimics vacillate between engagement and detachment. In contrast to the anorexic, who avoids the issues of rejection, intimacy and sexuality, the bulimic is intensely aware of her needs for intimacy, but fears them. The bulimic becomes dependent upon men to validate her self-worth (as she did with her family). Again, as in the past, self-worth is measured in terms of appearance and achievement. These relationships with men are often frustrating and unrewarding.

The bulimic infrequently experiences a distortion in

body image and is usually within 10 to 15 pounds of normal weight. She tends to be gregarious, sociable, and an extrovert, but experiences intermittent periods of detachment and social isolation. In addition, bulimics are aware of their abnormal eating patterns and are demoralized and embarrassed by their binge behavior.

MEDICAL COMPLICATIONS IN EATING DISORDERS

There are a variety of physical signs and symptoms that may develop in persons with eating disorders. These may be due to the effects of one or more conditions, each of which are addressed briefly below:

1. Calorie deprivation and weight loss
2. Particular methods of weight control or reduction
3. Accompanying psychological states (i.e. depression, anxiety, etc.)

The more common physical changes that accompany weight loss in anorexia nervosa are shown in Figure A. These changes vary from individual to individual and are more pronounced with severe weight loss.

The various methods employed to lose weight are often accompanied by physical complications. Since there is some overlap of complications, combinations of these methods dangerously affect potassium regulation and fluid balance. Several commonly-used methods and their accompanying physical complications are outlined in Figure B.

Potassium balance is exceedingly important. Potassium depletion, in addition to acid/base disturbances and changes in sodium balance, may severely alter the body's chemistry. Depression, irritability, and fatigue are common effects of decreased potassium levels. If severe enough, the depletion can cause loss of fine motor control, heart arrhythmias (irregular heartbeats), and possible death. The mortality rate for anorexia nervosa is anywhere from 5-10% and is often due to heart arrhythmias.

The third factor influencing physical signs and symptoms in eating disorders is the presence of an underlying psychological state such as depression or anxiety. Depression can be a side effect of the starvation state and is often present in persons with both anorexia and bulimia. For example, it is not uncommon for women under stress to stop having menstrual periods. Clinically, patients with anorexia nervosa often report cessation of menstrual periods (amenorrhea). Although psychological stress may be a factor, this may also be associated with the physiological stress resulting from nutritional and hormonal imbalances due to weight loss.

Psychological factors such as anxiety and/or depression can influence both sleeping and eating patterns. Depression may be accompanied by insomnia, with difficulty falling and/or staying asleep, and/or early morning awakening. Depression can also be accompanied by increased sleep (hypersomnia). Anxiety may affect sleep in a similar fashion. Both depression and anxiety may precipitate a change in appetite with either an increase or decrease in appetite and body weight.

There may be multiple physiological signs and symptoms that develop in persons with eating disorders. They may be due to weight loss itself, weight loss/control methods, and/or underlying psychological states. These signs and symptoms may be due to more than one factor. Medical evaluation is important in assessing any physical risks that may be present, particularly metabolic disturbances that may lead to the dangerous consequences of heart arrhythmia.

THERAPEUTIC ALTERNATIVES IN THE TREATMENT OF EATING DISORDERS

Individual psychotherapy is the foundation on which the treatment experience begins. However, successful treatment of the eating disorder patient is multi-dimensional and highly individualized. A variety of other therapeutic approaches may be employed including family therapy, couples therapy, group therapy, behavior modification, chemotherapy, hypnotherapy and in-patient hospitalization.

INDIVIDUAL PSYCHOTHERAPY

Individual psychotherapy is generally recommended for all eating disorder patients. Within this treatment format, the individual is able to begin exploring attitudes about weight, food and body image. As the therapeutic relationship progresses, the content of the sessions often shifts away from food and weight concerns. Typically, the individual discovers that she/he is experiencing difficulty in relationships with family and friends, lacks adequate means of coping with stress, and has limited self-awareness and self-esteem. Individual psychotherapy provides a sheltered environment through which the individual can explore concerns, test new behaviors, and receive constructive and non-judgmental feedback. This process promotes maturation, growth, and independence. The frequency of individual sessions is determined by the therapist and the individual. Length of treatment is highly variable and should be based on the individual's needs.

FAMILY THERAPY

Generally, family therapy consists of one therapist and three or more family members. In certain situations, co-therapists may be involved. In working with the family, the therapist has the opportunity to assess the impact of the individual's behavior upon the family and to observe communication patterns, the handling of conflict, roles within the family, family decision-making patterns, and family myths/ideologies/values. The therapist initiates interventions designed to improve overall family functioning which, in turn, facilitates the recovery of the individual. Again, the frequency and duration of therapy are mutually decided upon by the family and the therapist. Family therapy is often a useful adjunct for adolescents, and periodic family sessions may be helpful to the young adult who is struggling with separation from the primary family.

COUPLES THERAPY

Couples therapy is indicated when there is significant conflict in a couple's relationship, whether it is due to the personalities involved, the eating disorder, or a combination of the two. This may include the parents of an eating disorder patient, or the individual suffering from anorexia or bulimia and his/her significant other. The purpose of couples therapy is to strengthen the relationship bond and to assist couples in problem solving and successfully resolving conflict. Periodic couples sessions may be useful in identifying relationship issues and in engendering and providing support. As with individual and family treatment, frequency and duration of sessions are dependent upon the needs of the couple.

GROUP TREATMENT

Group treatment and support groups provide an arena for demystifying the disorder, diminishing feelings of isolation and secrecy, facilitating realistic goal setting, sharing successful techniques, expressing feelings and obtaining feedback from group members, and developing a support network both inside and outside the group.

Generally, support groups are free of charge, anonymity is preserved and members may enter or leave the group at any time. Support groups usually serve as an adjunct to therapy and are not considered primary treatment; rather, they provide support, information, and feedback which can augment the treatment process. Support group facilitators may be professional counselors, recovered individuals, or family members of anorexic or bulimic individuals. The foundation of support groups is the sharing of experiences.

Psychotherapy groups are most effective in the treatment of bulimia. They may be ongoing or time limited, membership may be closed or participants may join at any time, and the frequency and duration of sessions varies. A fee is usually assessed for this form of treatment. The therapy is conducted by a trained professional and the focus is on individual dynamics and group process.

Behavior modification groups differ from psychotherapy groups in the manner in which the therapist approaches the treatment process. The goal of behavior modification is to systematically eliminate self-defeating behaviors. Behavior modification programs may include the teaching of stress management techniques such as relaxation training, biofeedback, and assertiveness skills. These groups are run by trained professionals and a fee is assessed. Frequency and duration of sessions is variable.

CHEMOTHERAPY

Chemotherapy involves the use of prescription drugs to allay distressing psychological symptoms and augment therapy. Although there is much controversy about the use of medications with eating disordered patients, antidepressants may indeed be effective in the treatment of certain forms of depression which may occur in these individuals. In severely starved and malnourished anorexics, medication usually is avoided due to the increased sensitivity to side effects and potentially serious complications including cardiac arrhythmias and blood pressure fluctuations. In addition, drug kinetics and metabolism are somewhat unpredictable in a starved individual and unexpected complications may arise. Refeeding the starved anorexic may alleviate the signs and symptoms of depression, if present.

In considering the use of chemotherapy as an adjunct in the treatment of bulimia, the following issues need to be considered: the type of depression, the type and frequency of weight control methods employed (e.g. diuretic abuse, etc.); alcohol or substance abuse; and metabolic status (e.g. potassium levels).

Laboratory evaluations prior to initiating chemotherapy may uncover metabolic, nutritional, and pre-existing medical abnormalities. Standard medical practice dictates observing the routine precautions when prescribing any medications.

NUTRITIONAL COUNSELING

Nutritional counseling may be helpful in the restructuring and normalization of eating patterns. It may be particularly useful for the hospitalized anorexic who is attempting to gain weight. In addition, nutritional counseling and, in particular, meal planning, may provide a useful structure for the bulimic patient.

HYPNOTHERAPY

Hypnotherapy may be helpful in uncovering underlying conflicts and facilitating relaxation in the eating disorder patient. Hypnotherapy may be difficult to undertake with the anorexic individual because of the underlying dynamics of the disorder (i.e. need for control, rigidity). Self-hypnosis may be a useful stress-management technique for the anorexic and the bulimic.

HOSPITALIZATION

Hospitalization may become necessary for both the anorexic and the bulimic. Assessment for hospitalization should be made by a trained professional.

In general, inpatient care should be considered when:

1. Weight loss continues after a reasonable period of time in out-patient treatment
2. There is an absence of necessary weight gain after a reasonable period of time in outpatient treatment
3. The individual is unable to break the binge-purge cycle after a reasonable period of time in out-patient therapy
4. There is a metabolic crisis (especially hypokalemia)
5. There are signs of psychiatric decompensation (severe depression, suicidal ideation, self-destructive behavior, etc.)
6. The individual needs to be separated from the family or environment before healthy behavior patterns can be established.

There are several alternatives available for persons needing inpatient care, including (1) medical ward of a general hospital, (2) psychiatric ward of a general hospital, (3) psychiatric hospital, (4) eating disorder program or unit of either a general hospital or psychiatric hospital, (5) eating disorder unit of an addiction or substance abuse facility, (6) residential treatment program.

The inpatient program for the emaciated anorexic is generally multi-dimensional. It typically involves behavior modification, individual (and perhaps group and family) psychotherapy, and nutritional counseling. In addition, any of the above treatment modalities may be incorporated into individual treatment plans, as indicated. Duration of treatment is highly individualized and based upon progress in therapy as well as weight gain or binge-purge control. If an individual is admitted due to an acute psychiatric difficulty, the nature of the difficulty dictates the treatment approach.

Periodically, individuals may be admitted to the general hospital ward for correction of metabolic abnormalities that have developed (e.g. low potassium). These admissions tend to be brief. They are usually managed by the general physician rather than the psychiatrist.

A successful inpatient treatment program includes planning for out-patient treatment. Prior to discharge, arrangements for outpatient treatment should be made to promote the continued progress of the individual.

This is a brief overview of the treatment modalities available. Early detection of the disorder is important, but treatment may begin at any time. Successful treatment involves not only a motivated client (though treatment may begin before the client wants to change), but also an experienced therapist who has good therapeutic skills plus specialized training in the treatment of eating disorders. A successful treatment program is highly individualized and may be a combination of a variety of the treatment modalities reviewed.

Copyright 1984, Enright and Sansone. All rights reserved.

The National Anorexic Aid Society operates a Hotline: 614-436-1112. By calling this number you can receive information about eating disorders and about treatment and support resources world wide. NAAS Hotline is operated by staff and volunteers Monday - Thursday from 9am - 8pm and on Fridays 9am -5pm.

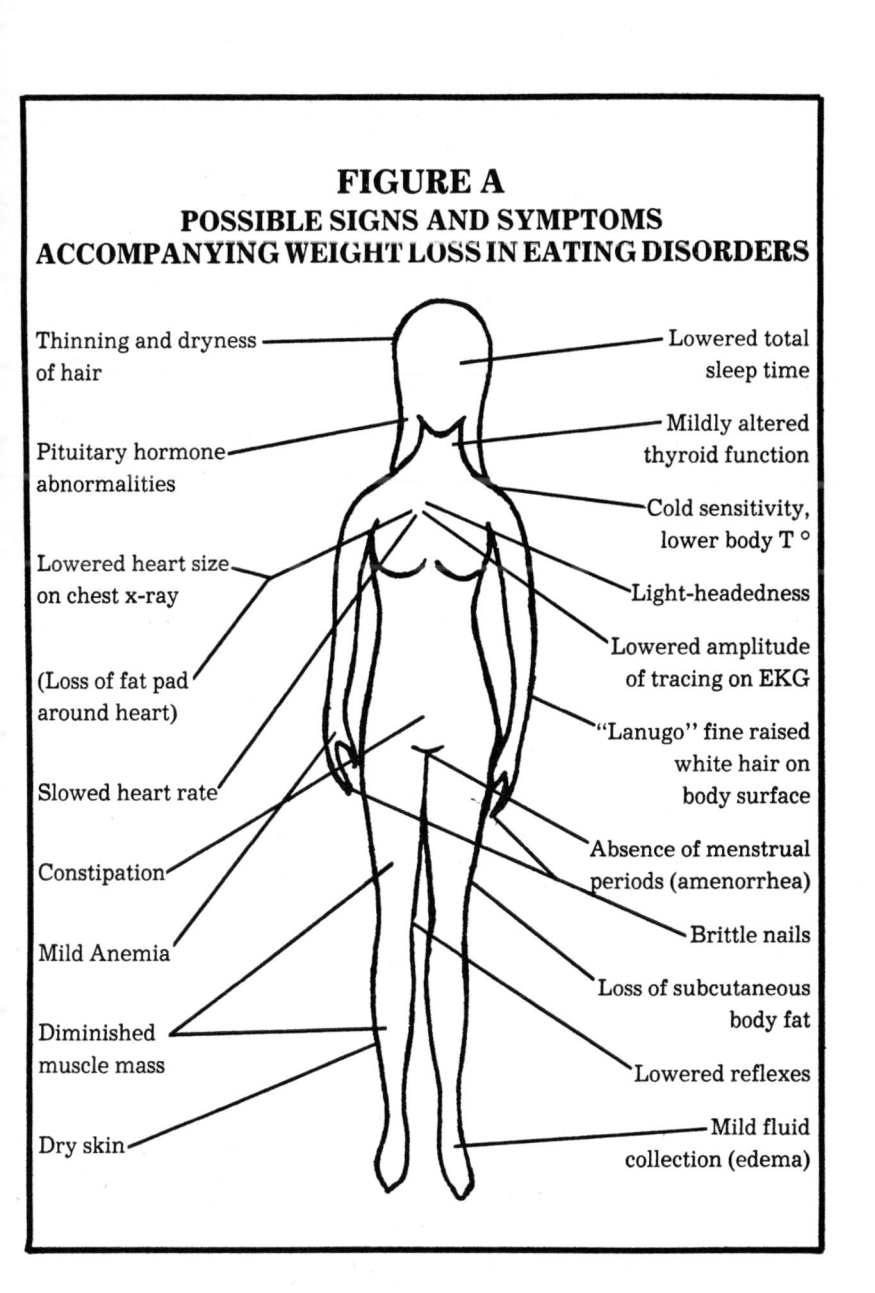

FIGURE A
POSSIBLE SIGNS AND SYMPTOMS ACCOMPANYING WEIGHT LOSS IN EATING DISORDERS

- Thinning and dryness of hair
- Pituitary hormone abnormalities
- Lowered heart size on chest x-ray
- (Loss of fat pad around heart)
- Slowed heart rate
- Constipation
- Mild Anemia
- Diminished muscle mass
- Dry skin
- Lowered total sleep time
- Mildly altered thyroid function
- Cold sensitivity, lower body T°
- Light-headedness
- Lowered amplitude of tracing on EKG
- "Lanugo" fine raised white hair on body surface
- Absence of menstrual periods (amenorrhea)
- Brittle nails
- Loss of subcutaneous body fat
- Lowered reflexes
- Mild fluid collection (edema)

FIGURE B
POSSIBLE MEDICAL COMPLICATIONS OF COMMONLY USED WEIGHT-REGULATION WEIGHT-LOSS METHODS

VOMITING

- Parotid gland enlargement (neck area)
- Erosion of tooth enamel and increased cavities
- Tears in esophagus
- Chronic esophagitis
- Chronic sore throats
- Difficulty swallowing
- Stomach cramps
- Digestive problems
- Anemia
- Electrolyte imbalance

DIURETIC ABUSE

- Hypokalemia (low potassium): fatigue; diminished reflexes; if severe, possible cardiac arrhythmia; if chronic, serious kidney damage
- Fluid loss: dehydration, lightheadedness, thirst

LAXATIVE ABUSE

- Non-specific abdominal complaints (cramping, constipation)
- Sluggish bowel functioning ("cathartic colon")
- Malabsorption of fat, protein, and calcium

Combinations of these methods can dangerously effect potassium regulation and fluid balance

NOTES

Notes

Notes

Notes

Notes

Notes

Notes

Notes